The Memoirs of (

The
MEMOIRS OF
𝕲𝖑𝖚̈𝖈𝖐𝖊𝖑 𝖔𝖋 𝕳𝖆𝖒𝖊𝖑𝖓

TRANSLATED WITH NOTES BY

Marvin Lowenthal

NEW INTRODUCTION BY

Robert S. Rosen

SCHOCKEN BOOKS · NEW YORK

Library of Congress Cataloging in Publication Data

Hameln, Glückel of, 1646–1724.
   The memoirs of Glückel of Hameln.

   Translation of Zikhroynes.
   Reprint of the 1932 ed. published by Harper, New York.
   1. Hameln, Glückel of, 1646–1724.   2. Jews in
Germany—Biography.   3. Germany—Biography.   I. Title.

DS135.G5H33813   1977   943'.044'0924 [B]   77-75290
ISBN 0-8052-0572-1

Manufactured in the United States of America

First Schocken edition published in 1977
   C9876

Illustrations

INTRODUCTION

by Robert S. Rosen

WHEN Glückel of Hameln sat down to write her *Memoirs* in the year 5451 (1690–1691), she could not possibly have foreseen that they would comprise one of the most remarkable documents of the second half of the seventeenth and first quarter of the eighteenth century and would, in time, become an invaluable source for historians, philologists, sociologists, and students of the literature of the period.

The writing had been undertaken as a kind of therapy after her husband's death, to get her through the long sleepless nights, to drive away "melancholy thoughts." She addresses herself to her children, assuring them that she is not writing a book of morals, but that she would put down, in seven little books, everything that had happened to her so far as "memory and subject permit." That she was able to see this project through is astounding, but what is even more surprising is the marvellous gift for storytelling displayed in these pages: the keen eye for detail, the ability to organize her material so that it flows naturally and effortlessly. Glückel, though she would not have known what to make of this, was an artist, and, as a true artist, gave more than she knew. In writing of *her* life, *her* family and business dealings, she has left us a portrait of an era. Better than any history text she instructs us about what it was like to be a Jew in Europe in her time.

Glückel was born in Hamburg in 1646, two years before the ugly and destructive Thirty Years War had run its course. When she was a little over two years old, the German Jews were expelled from Hamburg, and her family took up residence in nearby Altona, then under Danish rule. The Danish king, whom Glückel showers with praise for always having "dealt kindly with us Jews," granted the Hamburg exiles letters of protection. They stayed in Altona until the city was overrun by the Swedes in the winter of 1657–1658. They then returned to Hamburg where her father, Löb Pinkerle, was the first German Jew allowed to resettle. But Jews had no "right of residence" in Hamburg, dwelling there "purely at the mercy of the Town Council." The difficulties besetting Jews everywhere, the endless chicaneries they were subjected to, the need for special papers and permits of residence, form a constant backdrop against which the narrative unfolds. The situation in Hamburg where, Glückel tells us, "from time to time we enjoyed peace, and again were hunted forth; and so it has been to this day and, I fear, will continue in like fashion as long as the burghers rule," was by no means unique.

One of Glückel's earliest memories is the arrival in Altona of some of the survivors of the massacres in Poland by Cossacks under the leadership of Bogdan Chmielnicki. Starved and diseased, they arrived when there was as yet no hospital to receive them. Glückel's father, a *parnas* (president) of the Jewish community, put up at least ten of these unfortunate refugees in his house. Glückel's grandmother, then a woman in her seventies, could not be dissuaded from climbing the stairs to the garret several times a day to nurse the sick until she herself caught their disease and died within days. Glückel and a sister also became sick, but recovered.

At the age of twelve, Glückel was betrothed and at fourteen was married to Chayim Hameln, the ninth child of Joseph Hameln, who was the "perfect pattern of a pious Jew." The man seems indeed to have been blessed with all the virtues: modesty, patience, honesty. Not even rabbis, his wife tells us, prayed with as much fervor. He never failed to set aside a time for study, fasted on Mondays and Thursdays whenever he could, and wore himself out earning a decent livelihood for his family, which he loved "beyond all measure."

The early books are filled with scores of details, some remembered, others heard, about her and her husband's large family. Long before our current awareness of the importance of "roots," before the popular search to find out where we come from, Glückel wanted to be sure that her children knew "from what sort of people you have sprung, lest today or tomorrow your beloved children and grandchildren come and know naught of their family." To make sure that her descendants would not need to feel ashamed about their forebears, she spent much time promoting the most desirable matches for her twelve children. Her success in this regard put her at the center of the Jewish social life of her time. The sphere of her social and business activities spanned several countries—Germany, France, Denmark, Holland, Austria, and Poland—and included the cities of Altona, Amsterdam, Baierndorf, Bamberg, Berlin, Cleve, Danzig, Hanover, Hildesheim, Copenhagen, Frankfurt, Leipzig, Metz, Vienna, and others. She herself traveled widely despite all the hazards travel implied in her day. While Glückel does not dwell on major world events like wars and plagues, an echo of them finds its way into her recollections. In a most affecting way she touches on what was, no doubt, the greatest Jewish upheaval of the seventeenth century: the appearance of the Messianic pretender Sabbatai Zevi and his impact on the Jewish community. Many Jews, including Glückel's father-in-law, sold their homes and land, "for any day they hoped to be redeemed." Expecting to set sail for the Holy Land from Hamburg, Joseph Hameln sent two casks with provisions to the house of his son and his daughter-in-law where they stood ready for three years while the good man "awaited the signal to depart."

Mostly, Glückel records personal triumphs and sorrows: births and weddings, illness and death—the greatest shock of all being the death, in 1689, of her "dear friend," the "beloved companion" of thirty years, which is told in moving detail in Book Five. Glückel, widowed, with eight of her twelve children still unmarried, some mere infants, had to take on all by herself the burden of her husband's business, as well as the responsibility for caring for her family. She was then forty-four years old. In the ten years that followed she threw herself with enormous energy into the business world and provided dowries and matches for all but her youngest daughter, who was only eleven in 1699, when Book Five comes to a close. Then there is a long silence.

Much later, in 1715, Glückel takes up her *Memoirs* again. Her tone in the last two books is much sadder, and we soon learn the reason for that. Having been wearied by constant travel and become desperately afraid of failing in business and thus becoming dependent on her children, she had agreed to marry (in 1700) Cerf Levy of Metz, *parnas* of the Jewish community and the richest banker in Lorraine. Two years later, the calamity she had dreaded most did occur, and her new husband went bankrupt—

lost all his money and Glückel's too and barely escaped imprisonment. Cerf Levy died in 1712, a broken man, leaving Glückel in dire circumstances. But not till three years later does she yield to the entreaties of her daughter and her son-in-law (ironically the only match about which she had had some apprehension) and move into their house in Metz where she is treated exceedingly well and "paid all honors in the world." Glückel had retained her interest in public affairs and, her personal misfortune notwithstanding, found Metz to be "a very beautiful and pious community." Nor had she lost her touch in writing engagingly about matters such as the rift concerning the selection of a new rabbi or in relating a disaster like the one that befell the community when panic broke out in the synagogue, on the Sabbath of the Feast of Weeks, and six women were trampled to death. Glückel completed the seventh and final book of the *Memoirs* in 1719. Five years later she died, on September 19, 1724, at the age of seventy-eight.

Publication of the *Memoirs* was a long time in coming. It was not until 1896 that the great Jewish scholar David Kaufmann, of Budapest, published an edition in the original Judeo-German, in Frankfurt am Main, based on a copy of Glückel's manuscript made by her son Rabbi Moses Hameln of Baiersdorf. The copy was then part of the collection of Eugen Merzbacher in Munich. The original manuscript had been lost, but a second copy of it made by another Hameln was also utilized by Dr. Kaufmann. Kaufmann's edition (complete with introduction, index, and footnotes rendering some of Glückel's words, which betray the Hamburg dialect, into modern German) became the basis for all subsequent translations. Since Glückel's language is interspersed with numerous Hebrew words and phrases, snatches of prayers, and quotations from the Bible and Talmud, any translation presents inordinate problems.

The first of two translations into German was made by a descendant of Glückel, Bertha Pappenheim, and printed privately, in Vienna, in 1910, for the grandchildren and great-grandchildren of Benedikt Salomon Goldschmidt, who was also related to the Hameln family. This edition, which adheres closely to the Kaufmann text, includes some tables of genealogy showing the relationship of the Hameln family to several other distinguished German Jewish families. One of Glückel's better known descendants, incidentally, was the poet Heinrich Heine. A second German translation, slightly abridged and with critical notes, was made by Alfred Feilchenfeld (Berlin, 1920). It is to this edition that Marvin Lowenthal, whose English translation is being offered here, owes his "arrangement for dividing the first two 'books' and a number of happy suggestions pertaining to the order of the text." These slight departures from the Kaufmann text give a better balance to the first two books and to the work as a whole. Also, Lowenthal further abridged what he called the "theologizing" and omitted some of the borrowed tales Glückel incorporated into her narrative, like the story of Croesus and Solon, and shortened others. While such tamperings may offend some purists, they can be justified on the ground that they have resulted in a much tighter book. Nothing of Glückel's own story has been left out, and the over-all changes are minor, so that no one but the specialist ought to object.

Since Lowenthal's translation was first published forty-five years ago, there has been one other translation into English. This one, by Beth-Zion Abrahams, appeared first in England in 1962 and is a closer rendering of the Kaufmann text, though it too sees fit to skip pages of what it refers to as "really wearisome repetitious moralizing." What makes the Lowenthal translation particularly attractive and unsurpassed is its tone. It has admirably succeeded in capturing something of the spirit of the original by giving the English language a ring of an earlier period without sounding archaic. The notes appended to the text are based on those in the editions of Kaufmann and Feilchenfeld, but are in part Lowenthal's own. They are altogether helpful.

An abbreviated version of the *Memoirs* appeared in Hebrew, in Tel Aviv, in 1930, but curiously enough a translation into modern Yiddish appeared for the first time only in 1967. This edition was published in Buenos Aires in the series "Masterworks of Yiddish Literature," under the general editorship of Samuel Rollansky. The translation is by Joseph Berenfeld. Fragments of scholarly comments and a bibliography accompany the text.

The fullest and best treatment of Glückel's work to date, fittingly in Yiddish, is a superb monograph by the Yiddish poet and critic N. B. Minkoff that appeared in 1952. Glückel's *Memoirs* could, of course, not have had any impact on modern Yiddish literature since it was unknown prior to 1896. Its importance, as Minkoff rightly assesses, aside from its own contribution to Yiddish literature (it is the only extant pre-modern Yiddish memoir by a woman), lies in its revealing to us something about the impact of early Yiddish literature on the psyche of the Jew and especially on that of the Jewish woman. Thus we can trace in Glückel's book the influence—by no means conscious—of the *tehinnot* (devotional prayers, primarily for women, published since 1590 in little booklets); of the *musar* books (ethical tracts like the *Brantspiegel* published in 1602, mentioned by Glückel, and the *Lev Tov*); of the story books (like the *Maaseh Bukh* printed in Basel in 1602, containing some 250 moral tales deriving from various sources—the Talmud, medieval Jewish legends, mystic works and secular tales and legends); and of the *Tzenah Urenah,* a Yiddish Bible paraphrase interlaced with parables, allegories, and moral exhortations which, from its first publication in 1616 down to our own century, has been the indispensable companion of every pious Jewish woman.

The influence of the *tehinnah* can be felt most clearly in those parts of the book which relate the saddest episodes in Glückel's life—the death of her first husband, the disappointment of the second marriage. It is there that the subjective, intimate, and lyrical quality of *tehinnot* colors the tone and mood of the narrative.

Even more pervasive was the influence of *musar* literature. It should not surprise us that Glückel was incapable of avoiding the moralizing element despite the assertion that hers "will not be a book of morals." Her genuinely religious outlook on life. her belief in the rightness of God's judgments, her deep piety, color her descriptions of people and situations. The stories she uses by way of illustration—many of which revolve around the theme of sudden reversal of fortune—are meant to serve a moral purpose, even as, at the same time, they reveal a very strong writing impulse.

That Glückel had extraordinary writing talent can be seen not so much in the stories she retells, stories deriving from the *Maaseh Bukh* and other sources, but in the episodes from her own life—a bizarre incident after her stepsister's death, recollections of the plague, arduous journeys, wedding arrangements, business transactions— which offer us a profound insight into her time.

But what interest, aside from the historical, does Glückel's book hold for us today? To those who profess scorn for what they perceive as Jewish materialism and middle-classness, the book reveals the roots of those qualities, reveals the life-and-death matters that built those traits into Jewish life. A limited economy forced Jews in Europe into certain business activities that were more frequently fraught with danger than they were profitable. A respect for money was vital for their physical survival: near-ruinous taxes were levied on Jewish communities and on Jews individually in connection with every aspect of their personal and business lives. But on the scale of values, as Glückel's *Memoirs* reveals, material wealth for its own sake did not rank very high. Here is how Glückel instructs her children:

> The best thing for you, my children, is to serve God from the heart, without falsehood or sham, not giving out to people that you are one thing while, God forbid, in your heart you are another. Say your prayers with awe and devotion. During the time for prayers, do not stand about and talk of other things. While prayers are being offered to the Creator of the world, hold it a great sin to engage another man in talk about an entirely different matter—shall God be kept waiting until you have finished your business?
>
> Moreover, put aside a fixed time for the study of the Torah as best you know how. Then diligently go about your business, for providing your wife and children a decent livelihood is likewise a *mitzvah*—the command of God and the duty of man.

What does Glückel's example teach us about the role of women in Jewish life? We learn early that her husband "took advice from no one else, and did nothing without our talking it over together." On his deathbed Chayim Hameln did not hesitate when asked whether he had any last wishes. "None," he replied, "my wife knows everything. She shall do as she has always done." Truly remarkable that this woman who had given birth to thirteen children should have been involved in every aspect of her husband's far-flung business and that she was so much at home in the world. Not that she was entirely uncomplaining. Writing about a phase of her life in summary, toward the end of the fourth book, she says: "What, indeed, shall I write of the gaps betweentimes? Every two years I had a baby, I was tormented with worries as everyone is with a little house full of children, God be with them! and I thought myself more heavily burdened than anyone else in the world and that no one suffered from their children as much as I. Little I knew, poor fool, how fortunate I was when I seated my children 'like olive plants round about my table.'" No wonder then the general admiration and the assessment of her as the traditional "woman of valor." She was throughout a loving daughter, a devoted wife, the prototypical self-sacrificing Jewish mother, a woman of great warmth and strength—a strength that can only come from a totally integrated personality. She conveys, because she dominates these *Memoirs,* the impression that she moved on an equal footing with men.

We certainly have no right to expect that Glückel would challenge the laws that govern the roles assigned to men and women in the performance of religious duties and obligations. A poignant reminder of how inconvenient the

laws concerning ritual purity can be is given in the beginning of the fifth book when Glückel's husband's condition
is recognized as hopeless and he only has a few hours to
live. Glückel asks him: "Dearest heart, shall I embrace
you—I am unclean?" And he answers: "God forbid, my
child—it will not be long before you take your cleansing
[ritual bath that orthodox women take after menstruation
and childbirth]." It was, as Glückel adds, too late then. Is
there an implication in Glückel's question that a stricture
that has remained one of the more troubling ones for
Jewish women be ignored? Viewed from the perspective
of history, the Glückel who emerges from this self-
portrait, far from appearing to be a relic of the past, leaps
out at us a modern.

Much has happened in the forty-five years since this
book was first presented to English readers. Reviewing the
book for *The New York Times,* Florence Kelly then wrote:
"In Glückel's day it needed shrewdness and alertness to be
a Jew in Europe and escape disaster, and she has many a
tale to tell of one or another of her own and her husband's
relatives and friends cut down in the midst of prosperity
and apparent favor at court." This was in 1932. We know
that even shrewdness and alertness could not stave off disaster if you were a Jew in Europe after 1933. And we
wonder how many of Glückel's descendants in Germany,
Austria, and France were among those cut down in our
enlightened century, which saw an end of Jewish communities that had existed for centuries in cities like Hamburg, Altona, Frankfurt, Hildesheim, Berlin, and Vienna.
And so we read these *Memoirs* with an attention which
contemporary history has tragically sharpened. Yet for the
most part we shall find ourselves agreeing with David

Kaufmann who had first brought Glückel's manuscript to the light of day. "It is not a grave which this book reveals, but a human heart!" The re-issuance of the *Memoirs* at this time is most welcome.

1977   R.R.

The Memoirs of Glückel of Hameln

BOOK ONE

IN MY great grief and for my heart's ease I begin this book the year of Creation 5451 [1690-91] —God soon rejoice us and send us His redeemer!

I began writing it, dear children, upon the death of your good father, in the hope of distracting my soul from the burdens laid upon it, and the bitter thought that we have lost our faithful shepherd. In this way I have managed to live through many wakeful nights, and springing from my bed shortened the sleepless hours.

This, dear children, will be no book of morals. Such I could not write, and our sages have already written many. Moreover, we have our holy Torah in which we may find and learn all that we need for our journey through this world to the world to come. It is like a rope which the great and gracious God has thrown to us as we drown in the stormy sea of life, that we may seize hold of it and be saved.

The kernel of the Torah is, Thou shalt love thy neighbour as thyself.[1] But in our days we seldom find it so, and few are they who love their fellow-men with all their heart—on the contrary, if a man can contrive to ruin his neighbour, nothing pleases him more.

The best thing for you, my children, is to serve God from your heart, without falsehood or sham, not giving out to people that you are one thing while, God forbid, in your heart you are another. Say your prayers with awe and devotion. During the time for prayers, do not stand about and talk of other things.[2] While prayers are being offered to the Creator of the world, hold it a great sin to engage another man in talk about an entirely different matter—shall God Almighty be kept waiting until you have finished your business?

Moreover, put aside a fixed time for the study of the Torah, as best you know how.[3] Then diligently go about your business, for providing your wife and children a decent livelihood is likewise a *mitzvah*—the command of God and the duty of man. We should, I say, put ourselves to great pains for our children, for on this the world is built, yet we must understand that if children did as much for their parents, the children would quickly tire of it.

A bird once set out to cross a windy sea with its three fledglings. The sea was so wide and the wind so strong, the father bird was forced to carry his young, one by one, in his strong claws. When he was half-way across with the first fledgling the wind turned to a gale, and he said, «My child, look how I am struggling and risking my life in your behalf. When you are grown up, will you do as much for me and provide for my old age?» The fledgling replied, «Only bring me to safety, and when you are old I shall do everything you ask of me.» Whereat the father bird dropped his child into the sea, and it drowned, and he said, «So shall it be done to such a liar as you.» Then the father bird returned to shore, set forth with his second fledgling, asked the same question, and receiving the same answer, drowned the second child with the cry, «You, too, are a liar!» Finally he set out with the third fledgling, and when he asked the same question, the third and last fledgling replied, «My dear father, it is true you are struggling mightily and risking your life in my behalf, and I shall be wrong not to repay you when you are old, but I cannot bind myself. This though I can promise: when I am grown up and have children of my own, I shall do as much for them as you have done for me.» Whereupon the father bird said, «Well spoken, my child, and wisely; your life I will spare and I will carry you to shore in safety.»

Above all, my children, be honest in money matters, with both Jews and Gentiles, lest the name of Heaven be profaned. If you have in hand money or goods belonging to other people, give more care to them than if they were your own, so that, please

God, you do no one a wrong. The first question put to a man in the next world is, whether he was faithful in his business dealings.[4] Let a man work ever so hard amassing great wealth dishonestly, let him during his lifetime provide his children fat dowries and upon his death a rich heritage—yet woe, I say, and woe again to the wicked who for the sake of enriching his children has lost his share in the world to come! For the fleeting moment he has sold Eternity.

When God sends evil days upon us, we shall do well to remember the remedy contrived by the physician in the story told by Rabbi Abraham ben Sabbatai Levi. A great king, he tells us, once imprisoned his physician, and had him bound hand and foot with chains, and fed on a small dole of barley-bread and water. After months of this treatment, the king despatched relatives of the physician to visit the prison and learn what the unhappy man had to say. To their astonishment he looked as hale and hearty as the day he entered his cell. He told his relatives he owed his strength and well-being to a brew of seven herbs he had taken the precaution to prepare before he went to prison, and of which he drank a few drops every day. «What magic herbs are these?» they asked; and he answered: «The first is trust in God, the second is hope, and the others are patience, recognition of my sins, joy that in suffering now I shall not suffer

in the world to come, contentment that my punishment is not worse, as well it could be, and lastly,
knowledge that God who thrust me into prison
can, if He will, at any moment set me free.»

However, I am not writing this book in order
to preach to you, but, as I have already said, to drive
away the melancholy that comes with the long
nights. So far as my memory and the subject permit, I shall try to tell everything that has happened
to me from my youth upward. Not that I wish to
put on airs or pose as a good and pious woman. No,
dear children, I am a sinner. Every day, every
hour, and every moment of my life I have sinned,
nearly all manner of sins. God grant I may find the
means and occasion for repentance. But, alas, the
care of providing for my orphaned children, and
the ways of the world, have kept me far from that
state.

If God wills that I may live to finish them, I
shall leave you my Memoirs in seven little books.
And so, as it seems best, I shall begin now with my
birth.

1

My good mother brought me into the world, the
year of Creation 5407 [1646-47], in this city of
Hamburg. Even if our sages say, «it is better not to
be born,»[5] meaning that men have so much to endure in this sinful world, still I thank and praise

my Creator that He made me according to His will and beg Him to take me under His holy charge.

My father gave his children, girls and boys, a secular as well as a religious education. And whoever came hungry to my father's house went forth fed and satisfied.

Before I was three years old, the German Jews, I am told, were all driven out of Hamburg. Thereupon they settled in Altona which belonged to the King of Denmark, who readily gave them letters of protection. This city of Altona lies barely a quarter of an hour from Hamburg.

About twenty-five Jewish families were previously settled in Altona, where we had our synagogue and cemetery. After we newcomers had remained there for some time, we finally succeeded with great difficulty in persuading the authorities of Hamburg to grant passes to Altona Jews, so we might enter and do business in that city. Such a pass was valid for four weeks, it was issued by the burgomaster and cost one ducat; when it expired another had to be procured in its stead. However, if you got to know the burgomaster or his officials, the old pass might be renewed for a second four weeks.

This meant, God knows, a great hardship for our people, for all their business lay in Hamburg. Naturally, many a poor and needy wretch would try to slip into the city without a pass. If the officials caught him, he was thrust into prison, and then it cost all of us money and trouble to get him out again. In the early dawn, as soon as our folks were out of synagogue, they went down to Hamburg, and towards evening, when the gates were closed, back they came to Altona. Coming home, our poor folks often took their life in their hands because of the hatred for the Jews rife among the dockhands, soldiers and others of the meaner classes. The good wife, sitting home, often thanked God when her husband turned up safe and sound.

In those days we were hardly forty families all told. No one was very rich, but everyone earned an honest living. Chayim Fürst was the richest among us, with a fortune of 10,000 Reichsthalers, then came my father, of blessed memory, with 8000, others followed with 6000, and a few more with 2000. But great love and a close community spirit reigned among them, and in general they all enjoyed a better life than the richest man today. If a man were worth only 500 Reichsthalers, he could well be satisfied; and everyone was happier with whatever he had than nowadays when even the rich can never get enough. Of them, indeed, it is said: none dies seeing the half of his wishes fulfilled.[6] As for my father, no man had a greater trust in God; and if it hadn't been for the gout, he would have further increased his fortune. But,

as it was, he was able to set up his children in a
decent respectable style.

When I was about ten years old, war broke out
between the Swedes and the King of Denmark,
God heighten his fame![7] There is little new I can
tell of it, for I was still a child and forced to remain at my studies. I do remember we had the
coldest winter known for fifty years; and it was
called the «Swedish winter» because, everything
being frozen, the Swedes overran the country.
Once, on a Sabbath, the alarm went forth: «The
Swedes are coming!» It was early in the morning
and everyone was still asleep. We leaped from our
beds, *nebbich*,[8] and ran fairly naked all the way
to Hamburg, where we took up posts of defence,
some with the Sephardim[9] and some with the
Christian burghers.

In this way we remained in the city a short
while without permission. Finally, my good father
was able to arrange matters, and he was the first
German Jew allowed to resettle in Hamburg.
Others followed suit, and soon almost all were
back in Hamburg again. Those who had always
lived in Altona continued, of course, to stay there.

Government taxes were light in those days, and
everyone regulated his own settlement.[10] But we
had no synagogue and no right of residence; we
dwelt in Hamburg purely at the mercy and favour
of the Town Council.

Yet somehow the German Jews managed to come together and hold prayers in private houses, as best they could. If the Council got wind of it, at least they winked at the matter. But when the clergy discovered it, they became intolerant and drove us forth, and then like timid sheep we had to betake ourselves to the synagogue in Altona. This lasted a good while, till we crept back to our little Hamburg prayer-rooms. So from time to time we enjoyed peace, and again were hunted forth; and so it has been to this day and, I fear, will continue in like fashion as long as the burghers rule Hamburg. May the Lord, in the abundance of His mercy and loving-kindness, have compassion on us and send us His righteous Messiah, so that we may serve Him with all our heart and once more offer our prayers in the holy Temple in the holy city of Jerusalem! Amen.

So the Jews, as I said, dwelt in Hamburg, and my father dealt in precious stones and other wares like a Jew who knows how to turn everything to account.

The war between Denmark and Sweden continued to increase in violence. Luck lay with the Swedes; they despoiled the Danish king of all his possessions, and advanced on Copenhagen, besieged it, and were like to capture it. But the Danish king withstood the siege, thanks to the loyalty of his counsellors and subjects, who stood by him through thick and thin. Moreover he enjoyed the aid of the Almighty, for he was a righteous God-fearing king who had always dealt kindly with us Jews. Although we lived in Hamburg, each of us had only to pay his six Reichsthalers tax to the king, and we were quits.

Later, the Dutch rushed to the support of the Danes. Their ships sailed up the sound, the backbone of the war was broken and peace ensued. But Denmark and Sweden have never been on good terms, and even when they declare themselves friends and allies, one is always ready to pick a bone with the other.

2

At that time my sister Hendele, of blessed memory, became engaged to the son of the learned Reb Gumpel of Cleves. She received 1800 Reichsthalers as her dowry, in those days a handsome sum, more than anyone had ever been dowered in Hamburg. Naturally her match was considered the most important in all Germany, and the whole world admired its excellence and the size of the dowry. But my father's business was good, and he trusted in the Lord that He would not forsake him, but enable him to do as well by his other children in their turn. He lavished hospitality on all sides, in a way unknown today among people who have fortunes of 30,000 Reichsthalers.

Jewish Costume in Glückel's Day

Bride and Bridesmaids
Fürth—1706

I must tell you now about my sister's wedding and all the splendid and distinguished people who came with Reb Gumpel. As for himself, who can praise him enough, the good and holy man that he was! A purveyor of goods to the Brandenburg court, no one today can compare with him for the honesty of his deliveries. But I really can't describe how *magnifique* the wedding was, and especially the rejoicing among the poor and needy.

My father was in no wise rich but, as I said, he trusted in the Lord. He left no debts and worked himself to the bone to provide decently for his family. He had gone through a great deal in his life and, already become aged and worn, he naturally hastened to marry off his children.

He was already a widower when he became engaged to my mother. For fifteen years or more he had been married to a splendid woman, of good family, named Reize, who maintained a large and fine house. My father had no children by her, but a previous marriage had blessed her with a daughter, beautiful and virtuous as the day is long. The girl knew French *like water*! Once this did my father a mighty good turn.

My father, it seems, held a pledge against a loan of 500 Reichsthalers he had made to a nobleman. The gentleman appeared at his house one day, with two other nobs, to redeem his pledge. My father gave himself no concern, but went upstairs to fetch it, while his stepchild sat and played at the clavichord to pass away the time for his distinguished customers. The gentlemen stood about and began to confer with one another in French. When the Jew, they agreed, comes down with the pledge, we'll take it without paying and slip out. They never suspected, of course, that the girl understood them. However, when my father appeared, she suddenly began to sing aloud in Hebrew, «Oh, not the pledge, my soul—here today and gone tomorrow!» In her haste the poor child could blurb out nothing better. My father now turned to his gentleman. «Sir,» he said, «where is the money?» «Give me my pledge!» cried the customer. But my father said, «First the money and then the pledge.» Whereupon our gentleman spun about to his companions. «Friends,» he said, «the game is up—the wench, it seems, knows French»; and hurling threats they ran from the house.

A few days later our gentleman appeared alone, repaid the loan with due interest, took the pledge, and said to my father, «You are well served and your money is well spent in teaching your daughter French.» And he turned on his heels and left.

My father raised the child as though she were his own. And eventually he married her off. She made an excellent match, being given to the son of Calman Aurich, but she died in her first childbirth. Soon after, her body was robbed and the shroud taken from her. She revealed the outrage to some one in a dream; the body was exhumed and the robbery confirmed. Immediately the womenfolk drew together and began sewing her another shroud. As they sewed at their task, a servant-girl ran into the room and cried, «Hurry, for God's sake! Can't you see *her* sitting among you?» But the women saw nothing. When they had finished, the body was decked in its new shroud. And she was never seen again, but slept in peace.

3

Following the death of his first wife, my father married my mother, who was then a fatherless child. My dear good mother, long may she live! has often told me how upon the death of her father, she and her good mother Mata, of blessed memory, were left alone and in need. I too knew my grandmother, and there never lived a more pious woman nor a wiser.

Her husband, my grandfather Nathan Melrich, lived in Detmold, a fine distinguished man, and very rich. Eventually he was expelled from Detmold and moved with his wife and children to Altona. At that time, barely ten Jewish families had settled there, all of them newcomers.

Altona did not yet belong to the kingdom of Denmark. It was held by the county of Pinneberg, part of the possessions of the Count of Schaumburg. When later on the count died without heir, it fell into the hands of Denmark.

Nathan Spanier was the first to secure permission for Jews to settle in Altona. But they came singly, in small number. Among them Nathan Spanier managed to settle his son-in-law Loeb, formerly of Hildesheim.

Loeb was far from being a rich man, yet he succeeded in marrying off his children nicely, as people used to in those days. Esther, his wife, was a fine, pious, upright person, and an excellent business woman. It was she who really provided for the family and who journeyed every year to the Kiel «Change,» or Fair. To tell the truth, she didn't have to burden herself with many wares, because formerly people were satisfied with a small turnover. She was a clever talker, and God gave her favour in the eyes of all who looked upon her; the ladies among the Holstein nobility delighted in her.

Loeb Hildesheim and his wife were able to give their children dowries of only 300 or 400 Reichsthalers, yet they procured rich sons-in-law, such as Elijah Ballin, a man worth 30,000 Reichsthalers, Moses Goldzieher, and others. Their son Moses was a rich and substantial man to the end of his days; their son Lipmann, although not so rich, was well-to-do and lived comfortably, and so did their other children. I am writing this to show you that big dowries do not always mean everything, as you can see from the days when people sometimes furnished small dowries to children who in the end became very rich.

But to return to my subject—when my grandfather Nathan Melrich was driven out of Detmold, he settled in the house of Loeb Hildesheim and brought with him his great riches. Esther, Loeb's wife, has told me wonderful things about these treasures. He had coffers all filled with gold chains and jewelry, and whole bags of pearls, so I do not suppose that in those days there was as rich a man for a hundred miles around.

But, alas, it was not for long. The plague, God shield us! broke out and carried off my grandfather and a number of his children. Destitute, my grandmother and two unmarried children fled from the house. The poor woman has often told me of her sufferings. They lacked even a bed, and had to build themselves shelter for the night out of boards and rubble. Her one married daughter could give no aid; and Mordecai, her married son, who had been making a good living, was taken by the plague, together with his wife and child.

My beloved grandmother, with her two orphans, found herself in bitter need, and literally slunk from house to house «until the wrath be overpast.»[11] When the plague somewhat subsided, she sought to air out her house and live in it again. But she found it almost bare; the best things were gone. Neighbours had stripped the very planks from the floor and had wrecked what they could not take. They had shorn her of nearly everything, and but a few odds and ends remained for her and her orphaned children.

What should she do? A few unredeemed pledges lay still at hand, and with these my good grandmother eked out her living. In this way she meagrely provided for the two children, my aunt Ulk (Ulrica) and my mother Bela, long may she live.

At length the good woman managed to scrape together enough to marry off her daughter Ulk. The bridegroom's father, Reb Hanau, a prominent man in his day, bore the rabbinical title *Morenu* [Our Master] and held, I think, the position of state rabbi of Friesland. Later he settled in Altona as rabbi of the community. The groom, Elias Cohen, received from his father a dowry of 500 Reichsthalers, and lucky in everything he undertook, in a short while he amassed a large fortune. But, alas, he died young, even before he was forty. If God had spared his life, he would have become a big man, for God had endowed him with good luck. If he so much as picked up—pardon the expression!—a piece of dung, it turned to gold in his hands. But, alas, the stroke of fate overtook him.

Some time before this, strife broke loose over the presidency of the community. For many years

my father, of blessed memory, had been *parnas*
[president]. Elias Cohen, however, was younger
and daily growing richer; he had a good head and
he came from a good family. So he said to himself,
and he didn't mind it being overheard, «Why
shouldn't I make as good a *parnas* as my brother-
in-law Loeb? I am as clever and as rich, and don't
I come from as good a family?» But about then
God, who had set his term and fate, carried him off.

While he lived, however, the community was
wrought on edge; and as things go in this world,
all sides found their supporters. And then the community was sorely stricken. First *Parnas* Fiebel-
mann died. Then Chayim Fürst, also *parnas* and
the richest man in the community, died. After
him, Abraham the *Shamash* [beadle] laid himself
down and died. With his last breath he said, «I am
called as witness before the court of Heaven.»
Chayim Fürst's son Solomon, likewise a *parnas*,
likewise died—an excellent man and a great student
of Talmud. And then others whom I've forgotten.
So God brought to an end the strife among the
parnassim.

But to return to my grandmother Mata—after
she had married off my aunt Ulk and set her up
housekeeping, she had nothing left for herself. And
there was still my mother to think of, a little girl
of eleven years. So she went to live with her other
married daughter, Glück, the wife of Jacob Ree.

Though far from rich, Jacob Ree had a going business which allowed him to dower his children with 400 or 500 Reichsthalers. These sums, comparatively modest as they were, procured him remarkable matches, all fine young sons-in-law out of the best families.

Now after my grandmother had lived for a time with her daughter, something arose—who knows? perhaps her many bereft grandchildren proved too importunate, or perhaps the natural differences between mother and daughter set them apart; anyhow, my grandmother finally took my mother and moved to my aunt Ulk.

There they set about to earn their own livelihood. My mother had already learned the trade of making gold and silver lace, and God in His mercy saw to it that she received orders from the Hamburg merchants. At first Jacob Ree, of blessed memory, went surety for her; but when the merchants found that she knew her business and was prompt in her deliveries, they trusted her without surety. Next she taught the trade to a number of young girls and engaged them to work by her side, so that finally she was able to provide a living for her mother and clean, decent clothes for herself. Little enough, however, remained over, and often my dear mother had nothing but a crust of bread the livelong day. She never complained, but put her faith in God who had never forsaken her. To this day she has kept her trust in the Lord; I would I had her disposition. But God endows each of us differently.

4

[Immediately upon his marriage with my mother, my father brought my grandmother into his house and placed her at the head of the table.]He provided for her the rest of her life—seventeen years she remained in his house—and honoured her as though she were his own mother. With his knowledge and consent, my mother returned her the linen she had received from her as a marriage portion; altogether my grandmother found herself as well off as if she had been in her own home. May the Father of Goodness visit his merit upon us and our children!

About this time, the Vilna Jews were forced to leave Poland.[12] Many of them, stricken with contagious diseases, found their way to Hamburg. Having as yet neither hospital nor other accommodations, we needs must bring the sick among them into our homes. At least ten of them, whom my father took under his charge, lay in the upper floor of our house. Some recovered; others died. And my sister Elkele and I both took sick as well.

My beloved grandmother tended our sick and saw that they lacked for nothing. Though my father and mother disapproved, nothing could stop her from climbing to the garret three or four times a day, in order to nurse them. At length she too fell ill. After ten days in bed she died, at a beautiful old age, and left behind her a good name.[13] For all her seventy-four years she was still as brisk and fresh as a woman of forty.

It would be impossible to tell you all the things she said and prayed as she lay on her death-bed; and how she praised my father, of blessed memory, and poured out her thanks to him.

My father and mother, it appears, had given her every week a small sum, sometimes a half-Reichsthaler and again two marks, for her to buy and supply herself with things after her own heart; moreover, my father had never journeyed to a fair without bringing her a gift on his return. She used to put together and lay aside all these sums, and then lend them out against small pledges.

Now, on her death-bed, she turned to my father and said, «My son, I go the way of all the earth.[14] I have been in your house and you have cared for me as though I were your own dear mother. You have not only given me to eat and drink of the best and clothed me with honour, but you have given me money. As to that, far from spending it, I have saved and scraped it together, and loaned it bit by bit against small pledges, so that in all I have brought it to about two hundred Reichsthalers. Now who is fitter to receive it than my beloved son-in-law? For it was all his. Yet if he were willing

to forego it and turn it over to my two poor grandchildren, my son Mordecai's orphans? . . . but I
leave it to his pleasure, to do what he will.»

Judah and Anschel and all the children and sons-
in-law stood at her bedside.

And my father, of blessed memory, answered
her, «Peace, my dear mother-in-law, by God's will
you shall long be among us, and you will portion
out the money yourself, as you see fit. Gladly I
forego it, with all my heart; and if the Father of
Goodness restore you, I will add to it one hundred
Reichsthalers so the interest will increase, and then
do with it as you choose.»

When my grandmother heard my father, her
poor heart overflowed with joy, and she began to
bless him and my mother and her children with
every blessing in the world, and she told her praise
of them before all the people.

The following day she passed away in a gentle
sleep, and she was buried with great honour as
she deserved. May the reward of her merits be upon
us and our children and our children's children!

5

The community prospered during the presidency
of my father, so it could be said that they sat
«every man under his vine and under his fig tree.»
In its own name, it owed not a penny of debt.
I do recall, however, while I was yet a child, certain scoundrels rose against my father and his fel-

low officials, and sought to injure the community. Two of them managed to elicit letters from the government conveying them the right to be *parnassim* by royal authority. Now that they are dead and stand in judgment before the Most High, I will not name them, but everyone in our community well knows who they were.

God, however, destroyed their wicked plot. The *parnassim* and other leaders of the community, God be praised! quashed the whole matter. Then they journeyed to Copenhagen and reported everything to the king. He was a pious man, a lover of righteousness, so that, God be praised! all ended well and the wicked were cast down. What is more, it cost the community very little money. Our leaders, you must know, watched the interests of the community and its members like the apple of their eye, to keep them free from debt. Whenever a few hundred Reichsthalers were needed, the *parnas* advanced the sum from his own pocket, and then reclaimed it in small amounts whereby the community felt no burden. Heavens, when I come to think of it, what a blessed happy life we led compared to nowadays, although people didn't have half of what folks, God prosper them! possess today, God greaten and not lessen them! In their days and in our days may Israel be redeemed.

THE END OF MY FIRST BOOK

BOOK TWO

1

MY FATHER had me betrothed when I was a girl of barely twelve, and less than two years later I married.

The marriage took place in Hameln, and my parents together with about twenty wedding guests brought me there. Mail coaches didn't exist in those days, and we had to hire wagons from the peasants to take us as far as Hanover. There we wrote to Hameln for conveyances to complete our journey. My mother must have thought that carriages were as plentiful in Hameln as at home in Hamburg. Anyway, she figured that my father-in-law would send us nothing short of carriages in which to speed the bride and bridal party.

But three days later there appeared three or four peasant carts! Horses, too, or we should have had to trundle them along by hand. Despite her anger, my mother could do nothing about it; we plumped ourselves, Lord help us! in the little carts and so we came to Hameln.

That night we held high festival. My splendid

father-in-law, Joseph Hameln, of blessed memory, the like of whom you rarely see, raised a great glass of wine and toasted my mother. But she was still a little ruffled about the peasant carts.

My father-in-law sensed her resentment, and being a good-natured man as well as something of a wit, he said to her:

«Now please don't be angry; Hameln isn't Hamburg, we have no coaches, for we're just plain country folk. Let me tell you what happened when I was a bridegroom and set out to my own wedding.

«My father, Samuel Stuttgart, was *parnas* of all Hessia, and my Freudchen was Nathan Spanier's daughter. She brought a dowry of two thousand Reichsthalers and my blessed father had promised me fifteen hundred Reichsthalers, a fine portion in those days. Well, time come for the wedding, my father hired a porter, a fellow known thereabouts as the Fish. We slung the dowry over his shoulders to carry it to Stadthagen, my father-in-law's home. So I and the Fish set out together on foot, and trudged it to Stadthagen. Loeb Hildesheim was living there at the time, for he too was a son-in-law of Nathan Spanier. Well, when I drew near the town, a cry went up, ‹Here comes the groom!› Whereat this Loeb Hildesheim with some of the bridal party rides out to meet me. He was a real Hildesheimer, good family, people who live smartly at all times. After one glance at me, on foot, with my friend the Fish, he wheeled around and sped back to town and cried to my bride the news: ‹Your bridegroom, you know how he travels? —with a fish!›

«But now, madam, that I have got so far as to travel with a horse, don't be impatient, there's hope for me yet.»

At this, laughter and good feeling cleared the air, and the wedding was celebrated with joy and cheer.

Immediately afterwards my parents returned home and left me—I was a child of scarcely fourteen—alone with strangers in a strange world. That it did not go hard with me I owed to my new parents who made my life a joy. Both dear and godly souls, they cared after me better than I deserved. What a man he was, my father-in-law, like one of God's angels!

Hameln, everyone knows what it is compared to Hamburg; taken by itself, it is a dull shabby hole. And there I was—a carefree child whisked in the flush of youth from parents, friends and everyone I knew, from a city like Hamburg plump into a back-country town where lived only two Jews.

Yet I thought nothing of it, so much I delighted in the piety of my father-in-law. At three in the morning he arose, and in his Sabbath coat seated himself close to my bedroom and sing-songed his prayers; and then I forgot all about Hamburg.

The holy man he was, may all of us reap the reward of his merits, for his sake God spare us further trials and suffer us not to come to shame or sin!

2

His virtues shone again in his fine God-fearing children. Moses, the eldest son, was a splendid youth, who rode to his wedding, dowry and all, accompanied by the learned Reb Mosheh and a servant nicknamed Bullet-proof Jacob. As they approached Bremervörde, robbers fell upon and despoiled them, and left all three covered with wounds. They were carried to a neighbouring village; and the doctors and chirurgeons summoned to their aid were of the opinion that Reb Mosheh and the bridegroom would survive, but Jacob, riddled with shot, they held as good as dead. However, two days later they both died, and Jacob eventually recovered. That is how he came to be called Bullet-proof Jacob.

You may well imagine the pain and grief of the parents! Although redress for the murder was sought in many quarters, it proved in vain, and the murder remains unatoned to this day. May God avenge their blood!

I knew the second son, Abraham Hameln. He was as full of Torah as a pomegranate is full of seeds. So my father-in-law sent him as a Talmud student to Poland.[1] His prowess in Talmud earned

him a great name there, and he married in Posen
the daughter of a distinguished man, Chayim Boas.
After his wedding he continued to «learn» Talmud
diligently, and ever deepening his mastery of it,
he arose to considerable authority in Posen. But
some years later, when the Polish communities were
devastated by the war against Chmielnicki, he was
compelled to return, with his wife and daughter,
to my father-in-law's house, stripped of all his
possessions.

The birth of this daughter was something more
than strange. Seventeen years he had lived with
his wife and had no child by her. Then his mother-
in-law fell sick unto death, and bade her daughter,
my brother-in-law's wife, come to her. And she
said to her, «Daughter mine, I lie in God's hand
and am about to die; if I have earned any reward
in heaven I shall beg it be requited me in blessing
you with children.» The pious woman died soon
after. And fast on her death, my sister-in-law
found herself expectant; and in due time she gave
birth to a daughter whom she called after her
mother, Sarah. Seven years later she bore a son,
named Samuel.

Much could be written about Abraham Hameln.
My father-in-law set him up in Hanover, where
he found himself very well placed. But later he was
enticed from Hanover and induced to settle in
Hameln, to the hurt of himself and his children.

He was made all sorts of promises and offered a partnership, but nothing came of the promises or the partnership, God forgive them! My brother-in-law, Reb Abraham of blessed memory, was a great Talmud scholar and a wise man of mark; he spoke little, but when he said anything, the breath of his mouth was wisdom itself, and everyone stood agape to hear him.

My father-in-law likewise had a daughter, Yenta. He betrothed her, while she was still very young, to the son of Sussmann Gans of Minden-on-the-Weser. At that time Sussmann Gans had the name of a man worth 100,000 Reichsthalers. My father-in-law was out tippling with him, and the match was clinched over the wine. Next day, when Sussmann Gans had sobered up, he regretted the bargain. But my father-in-law was too well known for his probity, and what was done was done, so the match stood.

As both bride and groom were still very young, Sussmann Gans despatched his son to study Talmud in Poland. Soon after, Sussmann Gans died. He left no friends behind him who could have looked after his estate, so his fortune rapidly vanished. His widow, meanwhile, took to herself another husband, Feibisch Gans.

Some years later the young bridegroom returned from Poland; but instead of the many thousand Reichsthalers my father-in-law had figured on, he was worth a scant few hundred. My father-in-law was of a mind to break off the match, but my mother-in-law refused to hear of it, lest the fatherless youth be shamed. The young pair were accordingly wedded, and they lived for some years in Minden.

Then it came about that Feibisch and his wife married off a son of their own. Great wealth was displayed at the «spindle» feast,[2] and a handsome array of plate and utensils decked their table. Solomon Gans remarked the display, and no doubt recognized, besides, some of the plate as belonging to Sussmann Gans, his father; yet little enough had *he* received of his father's estate.

So he went into his stepfather's counting-room, and he looked about, and his hands fell on a little box full of written documents which he deemed his by right. But if I once begin, how can I ever end? Twenty sheets of paper would not hold what I could write if I told all that came of it.

The next day Feibisch missed the little box of documents and at once suspected his stepson. They fell to wrangling and went to law, of course, and my father-in-law along with them. The suit cost my father-in-law and Feibisch more than 2000 Reichsthalers apiece. For years they fought each other and carried the case to the higher authorities, and finally they put their very lives at stake. Once Feibisch had my father-in-law thrust into prison, and my father-in-law did as much by Feibisch a number of times. They kept at it till both of them ran out of money, although my father-in-law could have held out the longer.

At length, third parties intervened and insisted on summoning rabbis and rabbinical-court authorities from Frankfort, to settle the matter once and for all. The rabbis and authorities came, they pondered the case at due length, but they accomplished nothing—except to depart with fat fees. One of these rabbinical judges, from Gelnhausen, made off with enough to build for himself a handsome study-room; and he had painted on its wall three or four rabbis in their clerical hats, plucking the feathers from a goose [*Gans*].

Later, my father-in-law brought from Minden his son-in-law Solomon Gans and his daughter Yenta, and settled them in Hanover, where he likewise provided another child with the right of residence. Hanover was even then a town of considerable importance, and Solomon Gans was well pleased and achieved great wealth there. But his happiness was short-lived, for he died in his prime.

His wife remained a widow for some years, and, true young soul, wished never to marry again. But everything pointed so plainly to the rich Leffmann Behrens[3] as my new brother-in-law that the memory of Solomon Gans could no longer stand in the way. In truth, when Leffmann married my sister-in-law Yenta, he was not yet the man he is today. But God Almighty who lifteth up and casteth down,[4] holds all in His power. In working hard and spending hundreds to establish his children in Hanover, my father-in-law had thought to safeguard their future and the future of their offspring. Yet for whom had the good man sweated and toiled? For strangers. As it is said, they «leave their wealth to others.»[5] Alas, what more can I write? Everything falls out as it pleaseth the good Lord.

My father-in-law's fourth child was the learned Reb Samuel. He too had studied in Poland and married into a prominent family, the daughter of the famous Rabbi Sholem of Lemberg. He too settled there, and he too had to leave because of the war, and return empty-handed. So for a long while my father-in-law was compelled, in turn, to support him and his wife and children; and then he became rabbi in Hildesheim. It is not to be told, the pious and holy man he was; verily, he foresaw the hour of his death—all Hildesheim can bear out the truth of this.

His fifth child was the learned Reb Isaac, of blessed memory, whom I never saw. He lived in Frankfort-on-the-Main, and those who knew him can sing the purity of his soul and the depths of his learning. Few were his equal; he gave, it may be said, day and night to the Torah. He also reached no great age, hardly more than fifty, and he died rich and honoured.

The sixth child was his daughter Esther, the pattern of piety and womanly virtues. She underwent more than her share of troubles, yet her patience never flagged, to the moment she breathed her pure soul away. I need say nothing further of her, for all the world knows the excellent woman she was.

Loeb Bonn was his seventh child, an altogether worthy man, no great scholar, to be sure, none the less a sound reader of books. For a long while he was *parnas* of the communities roundabout Cologne, and he had his residence in Bonn. He died young—but in riches and honour.

The eighth child was his daughter Hannah, who might well be likened to her great and pious namesake. She died very young, and left no wealth behind her.

The ninth child was your beloved faithful father. I shall say nothing about him here, for you will find it all in its proper place.

I am writing down these many details, dear children mine, so you may know from what sort of people you have sprung, lest today or tomorrow your beloved children or grandchildren come and know naught of their family.

3

After our wedding, my husband and I remained for one year in Hameln. Our business went poorly, for Hameln was not a trade centre; and my husband did not wish to confine himself to money-lending among the country folk. From the outset of our marriage, he had bent his thoughts toward settling in Hamburg. And, as it is said in our holy writings, «The road a man desires, thereto he is led.»[6]

The first year of our marriage over, my husband would remain no longer. Even though my parents-in-law were both well pleased to have us stay in Hameln and, as it happens, offered us their hearth and home, still my husband willed otherwise. So, with their full approval, we left our parents-in-law and came here to Hamburg.

We were both children, young and inexperienced, who knew little or nothing of the business ways of Hamburg. But the great and merciful God who brought away my husband from his home and his father's house,[7] proved his ever-faithful staff. May God be praised for all the goodness He has bestowed upon us!

Upon our coming to Hamburg, my father engaged himself to board and house us for two years; and we lived with him.

Although my husband was a stranger, he quickly learned how things stood. At that time, the trade in gems was not as flourishing as it is now, and burghers and young engaged couples among the Gentiles seldom or never wore jewels. Instead, it was the fashion to wear solid gold chains; and gifts, if the occasion demanded, were all of gold. What though, to tell the truth, the gains were smaller than in jewels, my husband began by dealing in gold, and plying his trade ran from house to house, to buy up the precious metal. Then he turned it over to goldsmiths, or resold it to merchants about to be married; and he earned thereby a tidy profit.

However much my husband toiled, and truly the whole day he ran about upon his business, still he never failed to set aside a fixed time to study his daily «portion» of the Torah. He fasted, too, a great part of every day the Torah was read forth in the synagogue [Mondays and Thursdays], at least until he began to make long business journeys, with the result that even in his youth he became sickly and needed much doctoring. Yet, for all that, he never spared himself, and shirked no pains to provide his wife and children a decent livelihood.

So good and true a father one seldom finds, and he loved his wife and children beyond all measure. His modesty had no like, throughout his life he never once gave thought to holding public office; on the contrary, he would not so much as hear of it, and he was wont to laugh at people who hankered after such things. In brief, he was the perfect pattern of a pious Jew, as were his father and brothers.

Even among the great rabbis, I knew but few
who prayed with his fervour. If he were praying
in his room, and some one came to fetch him forth
where something could be bought up cheap, neither
I nor any servant in my whole house would have
the heart to go to him and speak of it. Indeed, he
once missed a bargain in this way, to the loss of
several hundred thalers. He never regarded these
things, but served God faithfully and called upon
Him with diligence; and He repaid him for all,
two and threefold over. A man so meek and patient
as my beloved husband will not be found again.
All that he had to contend with, and often, from
friends and strangers, he bore in patience. When
many times, in human weakness, I could no longer
contain myself, he laughed away my impatience
and said, «Foolish little woman—I put my trust
in God and give small heed to the talk of men.»
May his merits be our aid in this world and the
world to come!

4

Immediately on our arrival in Hamburg I became with child, and my mother along with me.
In good time the Lord graciously delivered me of
a young daughter. I was still a mere girl, and unused as I was to bearing children, it naturally went
hard with me; yet I rejoiced mightily that the Most
High had bestowed on me a healthy, lovely baby.

My dear good mother had reckoned out her time for the same day. However, she had great joy in my being brought to bed first, so she could help me a little, young girl that I was. Eight days later my mother likewise brought forth a young daughter in childbirth. So there was neither envy nor reproach between us, and we lay next to each other in the selfsame room. But, Lord, we had no peace, for the people that came running in to see the marvel, a mother and daughter together in childbed.

To fill this book out a bit, I must really tell you a pretty jest played on us. We lay together in a small room, it was winter, and my blessed father had a pack of servants; and even though the mothers and babies put up with one another nicely, we were rather crowded. So, to make a little more room, I used to sleep in my own chamber. However, because I was still young, my mother would not suffer me nights to take my child away with me. I therefore left the baby in our common room, where it slept and a maid lay near it. My mother bade me not to worry; if the child cried she would have the maid fetch it to me that I might nurse it, and then the maid would carry it back and place it again in its cradle. With this I was quite content.

Thus I passed a number of nights in my own chamber; and just before midnight, the maid would bring me the child to suckle. Once, though, I awoke about three in the morning, and I said to my husband, «What can it mean? The maid has not yet brought me the child.» «Doubtless,» said my husband, «it is still sleeping.» I gave myself no peace, however, until I had run into the room to look after the child.

I went over to the cradle, and I found it empty. I was sorely frightened, yet I did not want to scream for fear of arousing my mother. So I began to shake the maid in the hope of waking her quietly. But she lay in a deep sleep, and I had to begin screaming aloud before she could break off her slumber. «Where have you put my child?» I cried. Whereat she began talking half in her sleep, not knowing what she said. At this my mother awoke and said to the maid, «Where have you put my Glückelchen's baby?» But the maid proved too sleepy to reply.

So I said to my mother, «Mother,» I said, «perhaps you have my baby in bed with you.» «No, no,» she answered, «I have *my* baby in bed with me,» and she stuck to it as though some one wanted to make off with her baby.

Then it occurred to me to look for her child in its own cradle. And there it lay, soft asleep. So I said, «Mother, give me now my baby—yours lies in its cradle.» But she refused to believe me, and I had to fetch a light so she could examine it carefully. Finally I was able to make her accept her own baby, and bring away mine. By this time the whole house was aroused and everyone badly alarmed. However, fright soon vanished in laughter, and the word went round, «A little more, and we'd had to summon the blessed King Solomon himself.»

5

We remained altogether one year in the house of my parents. We were assured two years, it is true, but since my father's house was cramped, my husband had no wish to stay on; yet he did not take a penny for the second year's board. So we rented a lovely house, paying fifty thalers a year, and we moved with manservant and maid into our own home, where the Most High has mercifully kept us to this day;[8] and if God had not all too soon taken from me the crown of my head, I do not think there would have been a happier or more loving couple in all the world!

And so, as young folks, we set up our own home, and scrimped and pinched to be sure, but all as it should be, and kept up a nice decent house.

Our first manservant was Abraham Cantor of Hildesheim; we had him to look after the children. Later, he left us for some years and went into a little business of his own. Then he married a Hamburg widow, and when she died, a young girl from Amsterdam, and continued to live in Hamburg. We advanced him money and sent him to Copen-

TYPICAL JEWISH INTERIOR—NORTH GERMANY AND HOLLAND
Search for Leavened Food before the Passover

hagen; and today, it is said, he is a man worth 10,000 Reichsthalers or more.

When my daughter Zipporah was two years old, I was brought to bed again with my son Nathan. The joy my blessed husband had, and the beautiful circumcision feast he gave, cannot be told. May God grant me joy in all my children; now that I have, alas, no help or comfort more, save what I hope to have through them, I pray God Almighty to bestow His mercy and compassion on my plea!

With this I will close my second book. And I beg all who read it to put a good face on my folly in writing it; as I have said, it is born of sorrow and affliction. Praised be the Lord Almighty who gives me strength to bear it all!

With the help of the Most High, I will now begin my third book.

THE END OF MY SECOND BOOK

BOOK THREE

1

IT PASSES belief, all the strange things that can happen to us poor sinners.

I was about twenty-five years old.[1] My blessed husband worked manfully at his business, and although I was still young, I too did my share. Not that I mean to boast, but my husband took advice from no one else, and did nothing without our talking it over together.

Then it was that a young man named Mordecai, who had been with my brother-in-law Leffman in Hanover, came to Hamburg and stayed in our house. We found him to our liking, so we engaged him to travel for us wherever there was business to be done.

Being from Poland, the young man spoke excellent Polish, and accordingly we sent him to Danzig where we heard that seed pearls were plentiful, at that time a favourite article in the jewel trade. We gave him a letter of credit on Danzig for several hundred thalers and advised him somewhat on how to buy his pearls. If we had been able to dispose of stones in Danzig as well as buy them, we should have earned more; but in those days everyone was so set on the pearl trade, we gave no thought to other business.

So Mordecai proceeded to Danzig, and began buying pearls and sending them on to Hamburg. He bought, I might add, to good advantage and brought in a nice profit. But he had no will to remain in Danzig, for he was already of an age to marry. Back he came then, and was betrothed to the daughter of Tall Nathan; the wedding was stipulated for a half-year later.

My husband wanted him to return to Danzig in the interval before his marriage. But, alas, it was God's will that he had no mind to undertake the journey. «It is not six months,» he said, «until my wedding. The time would be up before I could go and return. I would rather travel about Germany buying-in wine.» My husband said to him, l«How in the world do you come to such an idea? I will have nothing to do with your wine business.» «Very well,» answered Mordecai, «I will buy on my own account.»

What though my husband pleaded and stormed, and even set Mordecai's future father-in-law upon him to dissuade him from his unhappy plan, nothing would deter him. The good man, it appeared, was fated to make place for another. For if God had spared his life, Judah Berlin and Issacha (Issachar) Cohen might never have risen to wealth.

So Mordecai set out to buy wine on his own account, since my husband refused to go into partnership; and he took off with him about 600 Reichsthalers. On reaching Hanover he left his money with my brother-in-law Leffman, who was to assign it to such towns as he chose to visit for his purchases.

Then he left Hanover to go to Hildesheim. But he was that close he did not permit himself to travel by post, or rather, God did not permit him. So he went alone on foot, for Hildesheim lies only fifteen miles away.

As he neared Hildesheim, less indeed than a Sabbath day's[2] journey from the town, a poacher fell in his way and said to him, "Money, Jew—or I shoot!" Mordecai laughed at him, for Hanover to Hildesheim is as safe as Hamburg to Altona. Usually the road is not deserted a quarter-hour on end; yet, alas, it had to be that no chance traveller strayed in view. The poacher now spoke up again, "Stinking Jew, what do you palter about—say yes or no!" With that he seized his gun and shot our Mordecai through the head, that he fell dead in his tracks. Thus the stout and honest lad came to his early grave; and instead of celebrating wedding feast and honours, he needs must creep into the black of earth—and oh, so basely! My God! when I think of it, my hair stands on end. For he was a good, pious, God-fearing child, and had God granted him his life he would have done great things; and it would have been to our own gain as well. God knows how my husband and I took it to heart, and our sore grief.

He lay in the road but a short while, weltering in his young blood, when people from Hildesheim passed by and found him in this wretched state. They recognized him at once, for he was well-known in the neighbourhood, and taking charge of him, they carried him then and there to his grave. The lamentation and wailing throughout the whole region is not to be told, yet what good did it all do? His young life was gone.

People in Hanover and Hildesheim wrote to us immediately, for they knew we were in business together and thought perhaps he carried with him funds of ours. But he had on him only a few Reichsthalers for current expenses. Although every effort was made in Hanover and Hildesheim to avenge his murder, nothing came of it. For the murderer, God blot out his name! took to his heels and was never seen again. May God revenge the blood of the stricken lad, together with His other saints and martyrs!

We were now left with no one to travel for us. A short while after, however, young Judah Berlin[3] came to Hamburg accompanied by a marriage broker, Jacob Obernkirchen, who was negotiating for him the daughter of Pincus Harburg. But the

match fell through; in truth, God had not des-
tined it. This Judah now became my house-guest,
for as the nephew of my brother-in-law Leffman
he was related to my husband.

Staying with us for some weeks, we found him
much to our liking. He was a pretty student of
Torah, he knew how to talk business, and he seemed
altogether a clever lad. So my husband said to me,
«Glückchen, what would you think if we took
up this youth and sent him to Danzig? I consider
him a likely young fellow.» I said to my husband,
«I had already been thinking of it; after all, we
must take on some one.» Whereupon we broached
the matter to him, he agreed at once, and within
the week he was off for Danzig.

He had brought to Hamburg his entire where-
withal, perhaps twenty or thirty Reichsthalers
worth of amber, which he left with my husband to
hold or to sell. Observe, my dear children, how,
God willing, He can make much out of little, how
Judah Berlin with a capital as good as nothing
achieved great wealth and so became a great man.

He now remained a while in Danzig, turning a
good profit and steadily buying pearls. Even so, he
did not do all the business he could. Credit, too,
was scarcer then in Hamburg than it is today, and
we were still young folks not overburdened with
wealth. Nevertheless, we kept him supplied with
letters of credit and occasionally sent him bills of

exchange, so he never lacked for money. After about two years he returned to Hamburg, and my husband cast up their accounts and paid him 800 or 900 Reichsthalers as his share of the profits. With this he went to Hanover, established himself thereabouts, and set out to get married.

Meanwhile, I was delivered of my daughter Mata, a very lovely pretty baby.

2

About this time people began to talk of Sabbatai Zevi [the Messianic pretender]. But «woe unto us that we have sinned»[4] and never lived to see what we had heard and nigh believed. When I think of the «repentance done» by young and old my pen fails me—but the whole world knows of it!

O Lord of All Worlds, hoping as we did that Thou hadst shown compassion on Israel and redeemed us, we were like a woman who sits in labour and suffers mighty pangs, and thinks once her suffering is over she shall be blessed with a child; but it was only hearkening after a wind.[5] So, dear God and King, it befell unto us. Throughout the world, Thy servants and children rent themselves with repentance, prayer and charity;[6] for two, yea, for three years Thy beloved people Israel sat in labour; but there came forth naught but wind. It was not enough we were unworthy to behold the child for whom we had laboured and in whom our hope was sure; we were left, in the end, abandoned. Still, my Lord and God, Thy people Israel despair not; daily they trust that in Thy mercy Thou wilt redeem them. Though redemption be deferred, yet every day I hope upon its coming. When it will be Thy holy will, Thou wilt in truth remember Thy people Israel.

Our joy, when the letters arrived [from Smyrna] is not to be told.[7] Most of them were addressed to the Sephardim who, as fast as they came, took them to their synagogue and read them aloud; young and old, the Germans too hastened to the Sephardic synagogue.

The Sephardic youth came dressed in their best finery and decked in broad green silk ribbons, the gear of Sabbatai Zevi. «With timbrels and with dances»[8] they one and all trooped to the synagogue, and they read the letters forth with joy like the «joy of the Feast of Water-Drawing.»[9]

Many sold their houses and lands and all their possessions, for any day they hoped to be redeemed. My good father-in-law left his home in Hameln, abandoned his house and lands and all his goodly furniture, and moved to Hildesheim. He sent on to us in Hamburg two enormous casks packed with linens and with peas, beans, dried meats, shredded prunes and like stuff, every manner of food that would keep. For the old man expected to sail any moment from Hamburg to the Holy Land.

More than a year the casks lay in my house. At length the old folks feared the meat and other edibles would rot; and they wrote us, we should open the casks and remove the foodstuffs, to save the linens from ruin. For three years the casks stood ready, and all this while my father-in-law awaited the signal to depart. But the Most High pleased otherwise.

Full well we know the Most High has given His word, and were we not so wicked, but truly pious from the bottom of our hearts, I am certain God would have mercy on us; if only we kept the commandment, «Thou shalt love thy neighbour as thyself!» But God forgive us for the way we keep it —no good can come from the jealousy and footless hate that rule our lives. Nevertheless, what Thou, Lord God, hast promised, Thou wilt like a gracious king fulfil.

With this I will leave the subject and return to my story.

3

While I lay in childbed with my daughter Mata, whispers spread that the plague, God shield us! was abroad in Hamburg. Presently it reached a point that three or four Jewish houses, too, were stricken; nearly all the inmates died and the houses stood almost vacant. It was a time of bitter suffering and desolation, when God have pity on them, it went hard with the dead. And most of the Jews fled to Altona.

We had by us some thousands of Reichsthalers in pledges, covering among others small loans from twenty to thirty, and up to one hundred thalers; for in the money-lending business, small loans of ten Reichsthalers or even five shillings cannot be refused. Now the plague had swept through the city, and we were constantly beset by customers. Even if we knew they were already infected we must deal with them, at least to the extent of returning them their redeemed pledges; and had we fled to Altona, they would have followed on our heels. So we resolved to take our children and go to Hameln, where my father-in-law lived.

We left Hamburg the day after Yom Kippur, and the day before the Feast of Booths we arrived in Hanover, where we put up at the home of my brother-in-law Abraham Hameln. Since the feast was so near at hand, we decided to remain there for the week's holy days.

I had by me my daughter Zipporah, now four years old, my two-year-old son Nathan, and my daughter Mata, a baby of close on eight weeks.

My brother-in-law Loeb Hannover prayed us to spend the first days of the festival in his house, where lay the synagogue. The second morning, while my husband was upstairs at services, I was still in my bedroom, dressing my daughter Zipporah. As I was drawing on her clothes, I saw that when I touched her she winced, and I asked her, «What be the matter, child?» «Mother dear,» she said, «something hurts me under the arm.» I looked and found that the child had a sore near her armpit. My husband, too, was bothered with a sore, which a barber in Hanover had covered with a bit of plaster. So I said to my maid whom I had with me, «Go to my husband—he is upstairs in the synagogue—and ask him who the barber was and where he lives. Then take the child to him, and have him lay on a plaster.» In all this I dreamed of nothing wrong.

The maid went upstairs, sought out my husband, and spoke with him. You must know that to reach the men's synagogue, one had to pass through the women's section.[10] As the maid left the men's section, my sisters-in-law Yenta, Sulka and Esther, who were sitting among the women, stopped her and asked, «What were you doing in the men's synagogue?» Whereupon the maid answered in all innocence, «Our little girl has a sore under her arm, so I asked my master, who likewise had a sore, which barber had been tending him, and I will take the child there as well.»

The women fell at once into a mad fright, not merely because they were natural weaklings in such matters, but coming from Hamburg we lay under

grave suspicion. They quickly put their heads together, considering what to do.

It happened that a stranger, an old Polish woman
who sat among them, overheard the talk and remarked their fright. So she said to them, «Be not
alarmed, 'tis nothing, I'll warrant. I have had to
do with such things a score of times, and if you
wish, I'll go belowstairs and have a look at the
girl, and I'll tell you if there is any danger and
what's to be done.» The women were satisfied and
begged her look the child over forthwith, so that,
God forbid! they run no risks.

I knew nothing of all this, and when the beldam
came to me and said, «Where be the little child?»
I replied, «Why do you ask?» «Why,» she said,
«I am a healer and I want to doctor the child, and
she will be cured in a twinkle.» I suspected nothing
and led forth the child. She looked her over, and
fled from her at once.

She darted up the stairs and cried at the top of
her voice, «Away, away—run and flee who can—
the pest is in your house, the girl is down with the
plague!» You can well imagine the terror and
screaming of the women, above all among such
chicken-livers.

Men, women and all, deep in their holy day
prayers, fled wildly from the synagogue. They
seized my child and the maid, thrust them out of

doors, and none dared shelter them. I need not tell you of our distress.

I wept and screamed in the same breath. I begged the people, for God's sake, «Think what you do,» I said, «nothing is wrong with the child; surely you see, God be praised! the child is hale and well. She had a running pimple on her head; before I left Hamburg I treated it with salve, and now it has gone to a little sore under her arm. If anyone were really stricken, God forbid! there'd be a dozen signs to show for it. But look—the child plays in the grass and eats a buttered roll as nicely as you please.

But it was all of no avail. «If it is known,» they said, «if His Highness the Duke hears that the like has fallen in his capital-seat, woe and woe unto us!» And the beldam thrust herself before me, and told me to my face that she'd give her neck if the child were not tainted.

What was to be done? I besought them, «In all mercy let me stay with my child. Where the child stays, there will I. Only let me go to her!» But they would not hear of it.

Presently my brothers-in-law Abraham, Leffmann and Loeb took counsel with their wives and bethought themselves what to do: where to put the maid and child and how to keep the whole matter secret from the authorities, for we all would have lain in mortal danger had noise of it come to the Duke.

At length they settled on a plan. The maid and child, clothed in old rags, were to go to a neighbouring village, not a Sabbath day's journey from Hanover. The name of the village was Peinholz. There they were to betake themselves to a peasant's house, and say that the Jews of Hanover had refused to shelter them over the holy days, being already overrun with poor, and had even refused them entry to the city. They must ask to pass the holy days in the village and offer to pay for the trouble. We know (they were to add) that the Hanover folk will send us food and drink, for surely they would not leave us in want during the holy festival.

Then they began negotiating with an old man, a Polack, who was staying over in Hanover, as well as with the Polish beldam whom I mentioned, to accompany the maid and child and see how matters fared. But neither of them would stir unless they were paid thirty thalers on the spot, to run so dire a risk. Whereupon my brothers-in-law Abraham, Leffman and Loeb held another consultation, and summoned the *melamad* [school-teacher], who was likewise a great Talmud scholar, to judge whether it be lawful to break the holy day by the payment of money. In the end they all agreed the money might be paid, since human life lay at stake.[11]

So in the midst of the holy festival we were forced to send away our beloved child and allowed the thought that, God forbid! she be tainted. I will let every father and mother judge what this required of us.

My blessed husband stood in a corner and wept and prayed to God, and I in another corner.[12] And, of a surety, God hearkened to us for the sake of my husband's merits. I do not believe that a heavier sacrifice was required of our father Abraham when he made to offer up his son. For our father Abraham acted at the bidding and for the love of the Lord, and thereby tasted joy even in his grief. But the decree fell so upon us, hemmed in by strangers, that it nigh pierced our hearts. Yet what could be done? We must needs bear all in patience. «Man is bound to give thanks for the evil, just as he gives thanks for the good.»[13]

I turned the maid's clothes inside out, and wrapped my child's things in a little bundle. I slung the bundle on the back of the maid like a beggar, and the child, too, I dressed in tatters. And in this fashion my good maid and my beloved child, and the old man and the beldam, set out for the village. You may know how we loaded the child with farewell blessings, and the hundreds of tears we shed. The child herself was happy and merry as only a child can be. But we and those of our own in

Hanover wept and prayed to God, and passed the holy feast-day steeped in woe.

The child and her companions meanwhile reached the village and were well received by a peasant, since they had money in purse—something one can always put to use. The peasant asked them, «Since this is your feast-day, why don't you abide with the Jews?» They answered, «Hanover is over-run with poor and we were not allowed to enter the city, but we know full well the Hanover Jews will send us food for over the festival.»

As for us, we returned to synagogue, but the prayers were through. At that time Judah Berlin, who had already done business with us, lived still unmarried in Hanover. Living there, too, was a young Polish Jew named Michael, who taught the children and who was likewise a sort of half-servant in the house, according to the German custom when folks had in a Talmud student to teach their children. (Later he took a wife in Hildesheim where he is now *parnas* and lives in wealth and honour.)

Anyway, as people were leaving synagogue, my brother-in-law Loeb had us called to dinner, for, as I said, he had invited us to stay with him, the day before the festival. But my husband said, «Before we eat, I must fetch food to the child and her companions.» «In truth,» said the others, «you are right. We will not eat until they too have something.» The village, I repeat, was nearby, as close as Altona to Hamburg.

So food was gathered together, everyone giving something from his own pot. The question now arose, who will take them the food? And everyone proved afraid. Then Judah Berlin spoke up, «I will take it,» and Michael said, «I will go with you.» My blessed husband, who loved the child dearly, accompanied them. But the Hanoverians would not trust him, for they thought, if my husband goes he will not restrain himself from approaching the child. So my brother-in-law Leffman went along too; and they all went together and took the food with them.

Meanwhile the maid and child, and their companions, for hunger and nothing else to do, were walking in a field. When the child saw my husband, she was filled with joy, and childlike, wanted to run at once to her father. Whereupon my brother-in-law Leffman cried out, they should hold in the child and let the old man come fetch the food. Of a fact, they must needs bind my husband with a rope, to keep him from running to his child, for he saw that she was hale and well and yet he could not go to her; whereat he and the child wept.

[So they placed the food and drink on the grass, and the maid and her companions fetched it away; and my husband and his friends moved off together.] This continued until the eighth day of the festival.

The old man and the beldam were provided with plaster and ointment and everything wherewith to heal the sore. Indeed, they healed it nicely, and the child was hale and well and pranced about the field like a young deer.

We now said to the Hanover folk, «How far will your folly lead you? The child, you can see, is healthy as can be and the danger is over and gone—let then the child return!» So they took counsel again, and decided not to let the child and her companions come back before Simhat Torah, the ninth day of the feast. There was naught for us to do but abide by it.

On Simhat Torah, Michael went out and brought the child and her companions back to Hanover. Who never saw the joy of my husband and myself and everyone present—we needs must weep for joy and everyone wanted to eat the child alive! For she was as lovely and irresistible a mite as ever you saw. And for a long while after she was commonly called the Virgin of Peinholz.

4

We remained in Hanover until the beginning of the month of Heshvan, that is, a week after Simhat Torah; then we journeyed with our children and maid to Hameln, where we planned to stay until all went well again in Hamburg.

But we enjoyed no peace, for we were heavily

involved in business, and had at the time in Poland a man called Green Moses. We learned from his letters that he had gotten 300 ounces of seed pearls and come with them to Hamburg, where he wrote my husband to join him. However, my husband did not set forth at once, but stayed on fourteen days in Hameln, for things still went badly in Hamburg and my father-in-law would not suffer him to risk returning there. They did not want us even to open a letter from Hamburg, and when one arrived we had to fumigate it twice and thrice over, and then as fast as we read it, cast it in the river.

One day, as we were sitting together gossiping, who walks into the room but Green Moses! It was in the cold of winter and he wore a hood over his head, but we recognized him on the spot. We motioned him to withdraw, for no one else remarked him, and had my father-in-law known he came from Hamburg, he would have driven him out forthwith.

In truth, sheltering a traveller out of Hamburg meant exposing oneself to grave danger from the government, even to the risk of one's life; and travellers were sharply scrutinized at all the town gates and public places.

We asked Green Moses, «How did you slip into the city?» He answered, «I said I was scribe to the bailiff of Hachem, a nearby village.»

What was to be done? There he was, and all the
pearls with him. We could not very well hide him
from our parents-in-law, and naught remained but
to tell them, and if it misliked them, that there
was no help for it.

Green Moses wasted no time in urging my husband to return with him and sell the pearls, that
he might be off again to Danzig and buy a new
store. Clearly, there was nothing else to do. Much
money was tied up in the pearls and, moreover, it
did no good to keep such wares on hand, for the
profit in them was small and like to be eaten up
by the interest were the wares not shortly sold.
So he decided to accompany Green Moses to Hamburg and set about to sell the pearls, and likewise
see how matters stood there, that I might take my
children back to our little nest. For I was mighty
wearied!

My husband, then, returned to Hamburg, and
with his pearls well worth 6000 Reichsthalers
banko[14] went at once to the wholesale dealers, especially the Muscovy merchants. He visited no less
than six of them, but no one made him a favourable
bid, so the gain would have been all too little.

He did not know where to turn next. It was now
the month of Shebat [January or February]. He
had to pay the bills of exchange which he had
used to buy his pearls. The Muscovy ships would
all set sail from Hamburg by the month of Ab

[July or August]; therefore, Tamuz [June or July] seemed the best time to sell. Since the present offer proved too low, he decided to mortgage the pearls, and he took 6000 Reichsthalers on them. He thought to get a better price for them in Tamuz. But far from that, letters came from Muscovy that war had broken out, whereat the merchants lost all stomach for buying pearls. And my husband had to sell the lot for 4000 Reichsthalers less than the previous offers, and pay a half-year's interest to boot. The first offer, I tell you, is always the best, and a man must watch and a merchant know to say «yes» as readily as «no.»

5

My husband now informed himself of conditions in Hamburg. Everyone told him all was quiet, and so it proved. Whereat he despatched me a travelling companion, our old friend Bullet-proof Jacob. A faithful fellow, he had but one fault: he loved to drink but could not hold his liquor. Well, my good man Jacob comes as far as Hanover, and he writes me I shall join him there with my children. The post, you must know, now ran from Hanover to Hamburg. I thereupon wrote to young Abraham Cantor, who had formerly served in our house, to meet me in Hameln and accompany us to Hanover. So we travelled together to Hanover and there we found Jacob.

He went at once to the local post-keeper, his boon drinking companion, and Friday he hired a coach, and we remained the Sabbath in Hanover.

It was vile weather and I had my three children with me. My brother-in-law Leffmann and his wife Yenta passed the entire Sabbath exhorting and begging Jacob to take all possible care of us, and only not to get drunk. He promised them, his hand on his heart, not to touch a drop more than he actually needed. But you shall shortly see how he kept his word.

Early Sunday morning we set forth from Hanover, I and the children, God be with them!—the maid and servant and my smart man Jacob. Now the post-keeper always accompanied the coach on this stage, and he was, as I said, Jacob's pot-brother.

Jacob settled us in our seats and made us comfortable, and then he and the post-keeper kept pace, on foot, with the coach. I supposed they would stretch their legs till we had passed the gate and then would take seat with us. So when we got beyond the gate I told Jacob to climb in, together with the post-keeper, that we suffer no delay and reach our night's shelter in good time. But Jacob said, "In God's name go your own speed! The keeper of the post and I are off to the village where there is some one he must see; we'll walk it as quickly as you can drive and we'll be up with you in no time." Their real purpose did not dawn on me. Langenhagen, the village Jacob spoke of, lay hard by Hanover; it straggled a full mile in length, and in the whole land there was not to be found better Broyhan beer.

So my good Jacob and the post-keeper settle themselves as nicely as you please in Langenhagen, and give over the entire day and a fair part of the night to Broyhan beer. I suspected nothing, we kept driving on our way, every moment I looked back for my good man, and of everyone I saw I never saw sign of Jacob.

We rode on until at length we reached the customs station about ten miles from Hanover. The postilion said to me, «Here you have to pay duty,» so I paid, and then urged him to drive forward, that we reach our inn at a decent hour.

It was storming fearfully, weather not fit for a dog, rain and snow together—near the Feast of Purim, I remember—and fast as the drops fell they froze. The children suffered bitterly, and I too. Again I begged the postilion to go on. «You can see for yourself,» I said, «how it storms and here we stand under the open sky.» But the postilion said, «I dare not leave until the keeper of the post arrives; he ordered me to stay here until he and Jacob overtake us.»

What could I do? We continued to sit there for another two hours, till finally the customs collector came and had us descend, and for sheer pity took us into his cozy room, where the children could warm themselves. There we passed still another hour. I now said to the collector, «Sir, I beg you, prevail on the postilion to depart, that I come with my little children to our inn before night falls. You see, sir, for yourself how it storms, so even in daylight we can hardly go forward—what then will it be in the dark of night? If the coach, God forbid! should turn over, we shall surely break our necks.» At this the customs collector ordered the postilion to leave straightway. But the postilion replied, «If I do, it's post-keeper Petersen will break *my* neck, and I'll not touch a cent of pay.» But the collector was a brave good fellow, and he forced the postilion to be off with us. «If those two drunken rogues ever come,» he said, «let them each take horse and catch up with you, for after all you'll be staying overnight in the inn.»

The postilion, then, drove on with us, and though the storm continued violent we reached the inn betimes, where we found a nice warm room and welcome. A snug room, it was overcrowded with drivers and travellers, yet everyone behaved kindly toward us, and pitied the children who hadn't a dry stitch on them. I hung up their little clothes to dry, and they were soon themselves again. We had brought good fare with us and the inn provided an excellent Broyhan beer, so after our wretched journey we were able to refresh ourselves with food and drink.

We sat up far into the night, expecting our two pot-brothers. But no one came. Presently I had made for me a bed of straw, whereon I and my little ones stretched ourselves. I was unable to sleep, but I thanked God I had brought the children to safety.

So I lay, lost in thought, until it must have been about midnight, when suddenly I heard a fearful uproar in the room. The keeper of the post had burst into the room with drawn dagger, and in drunken fury fell upon the postilion and purposed to kill him for driving off with us. Our host also came running in, and at length they pacified the post-keeper. I sat in my corner, *nebbich*, still as a mouse; the keeper a drunkard and a madman and I torn with anxiety, for I saw no sign of Jacob.

A bit later the keeper sat himself to food, and I saw that his fury had somewhat abated. So I went up to him and I said, «Herr Petersen, where have you left my Jacob?» «Where should I have left him?» he said. «He couldn't hold out, he's fallen under a hedge close to a pool of water, and by now I have no doubt he's drunk.» This sorely frightened me and I knew not where to turn. He was after all a human being and a Jew, and I was all alone. I begged our host to send, for me, two peasants to search after him and bring him to shelter.

So the two peasants rode forth, and a half hour from the village they found my good Jacob lying like a dead man, crumpled from travel and drink. His good coat and his little money were gone. The peasants set him on a horse and brought him to our inn. Although I was mighty angry with him, still I thanked God I was enabled to see him once again. It had cost me over six thalers. Well, I fetched him something to eat, and my fine servant who was to watch after me and my children, I myself must serve.

When day broke the hostlers brought up the coach, for us to journey forward. I seated my children, the maid and manservant, and I said to Jacob, he should seat himself too and not carry on as before. «Never again,» he said, «but I must take one look about the room to see if we have overlooked anything.» And I believed him.

But my good Jacob sat himself nicely again in the inn and began from where he had left off, to ply himself with drink. I sent the postboys in to fetch them both, for we had sat waiting enough in bad weather. The postboys began bawling what would happen, their horses would collapse, standing so long in the storm. But it was all to serve no good; the post-keeper was master and the drivers could do naught but wait. And again we sat for two hours, till both of them were roundly drunk and finally joined us.

Well, what more is to be written? We had the same story over again in every inn along the way. But with God's help we finally reached Harburg, about five miles from home. There my father and husband met us, and you can readily imagine our joy.

We took boat for Hamburg where, thank God, I found all my friends in good health. Indeed, few Jewish homes had been stricken while I was away. The storm was not altogether stilled, but here and there raised a flurry. The Jews, however, were and had been spared, God further shield us and deliver us in our need!

Once more we were in our beloved Hamburg after a half-year's absence which, we could reckon, cost us, what with the loss in pearls and interest, over 1200 Reichsthalers. Nevertheless, we praised and thanked the Most High that we and all of our own had been saved. Of the money we thought little—«Give me the persons and take the goods»[15] —moreover, God bestowed it on us again.

The people who had taken flight to Altona had one after the other returned to the city, and once more began to go after business. During the plague, you must know, trade had almost come to a standstill, for every door was closed against Hamburgers.

6

Some time later, while my husband was attending the Leipzig Fair he fell grievously ill. In those days Jews ran a terrible danger in Leipzig; if one among them, God forbid! died there, all his possessions were forfeit.[16]

Judah Berlin, who was likewise at the fair, tended my husband and nursed him with great care; and when he saw that my husband had somewhat recovered, he spoke to him as one good friend to another, and he urged my husband, who was far from strong in body, to give over these hard journeys. He proposed they should enter into partnership; he was young, willing to travel to the end of the world, and confident he could make enough for both of them to live at ease.

My husband said to him, «I can't decide in Leipzig. I'm not yet myself, and I fear to remain longer lest, God forbid! I grow worse. Since this is settlement week at the fair and at best little business can be done, I will hire coach and return home, and do you ride along with me. Once home, God willing, we can talk further, and my Glückelchen will be there to give us her sound advice.» For my husband did nothing without my knowledge.

Judah was by this time married. My husband had brought it about that he took for wife the daughter of Reb Samuel, my husband's brother, who provided a dowry of 500 thalers.

So my husband and Judah returned here together from Leipzig. Though still weak my husband did not need take to bed, and with good care he recovered quickly, perhaps in the space of a week. During this time Judah hung at my ear, urging me to persuade my husband to go into partnership with him. I felt I could not be responsible for my husband continuing his journeys abroad; if, God forbid, something had befallen him in Leipzig he would have lost both life and fortune.

In truth, his travelling mispleased me; I often suffered mortal agony lest he fall sick in Leipzig. Once he came back from the full tide of the fair without my knowing a word of it; I was looking out my door and suddenly up drives my husband—you can picture the fright it gave me! Another time he and certain Jews were returning from the Winter Fair in Leipzig, and they failed to reach here the day I had reckoned for their arrival. Instead, a woman who brought me the mail—letters, I remember, from Frankfort—told me she had heard, God help us, bad news at the post-office; a skiff containing two coach-loads of Jewish and Christian travellers trying to cross the Elbe above Hamburg had been crushed by an ice floe, and all on board were drowned.

I was, God help me, like to die; I began to scream

and wail, as you may well believe. Then Green Moses, whom I've already mentioned, comes into the room, and seeing my condition, asks me what has befallen. I tell him everything and beg him, «Take horse, in God's name, at once and gallop to the ford and see what's happened!»

Although he and others tried to talk me out of my panic, I could not control myself. So Green Moses rode off, and I flew to a man who rents out horses, and had him immediately despatch his servant to the ford, by another route. And when I hurried home in my anxiety and entered the house, there sat my good husband by the fire, warming himself and drying his clothes, for it was villainous weather. Everything the woman learned at the post was sheer lies.

Since worry and fright always came with my husband's journeys, I was ready to welcome a scheme whereby he could remain at home. So I did not look unfavourably on the partnership with Judah. And he kept at his proposals and offered the most tempting conditions.

At length I said to him, «Everything you say is well and good, but you see the size of our household and the heavy load we carry; we need more than a thousand thalers yearly to keep up our house, besides our business expenses, interest, and other necessary outlays; and I can't see where the money will come from.» Judah answered, «Is that your worry? I will give you, then, written assurance that if you don't make a thousand thalers *banko* a year, you have the right to dissolve the partnership.» Many other such assurances, too, he gave me, more than I can write.

I spoke now with my husband and told him of our talk, and what great business Judah boasted he would do. Whereupon my blessed husband said to me, «Words, my dear child, are all very well, but I have big expenses and I don't see how they will be met by a partnership with Judah.» At last I said to my husband, «We can try it for a year. I will draw up a little agreement and show it you, and then you tell me what you think of it.» So, at night, I set to work by myself and drafted a compact.

Throughout, Judah had urged and insisted we should relieve ourselves of all care and give our entire affairs into his hands, for he had ways and means, and knew where enough business lay to satisfy both of us. But I said, «How can we turn over all of our business to you?» Whereat he replied, «I know you have some thousands of thalers worth of jewellery which you won't sacrifice; so we'll agree that you shall sell or exchange them as you see fit.» This was one point in the agreement.

Secondly, the partnership was to run ten years, with an annual reckoning. And if the partnership did not bring in at least 2000 Reichsthalers a year, my husband reserved the right to dissolve it; without this clause we would have refused to enter into the arrangement. Then, should the partnership be dissolved, everything was to be sold, that each partner should receive back his money. Thirdly, my husband must once or twice accompany Judah to Amsterdam and instruct him how and what to buy, and Judah was to keep the purchases in his hands and undertake to sell them. Fourthly, my husband must put 5000 to 6000 Reichsthalers in the business, and Judah 2000; and Judah was to endeavour to sell or barter as best he could all the jewellery and other goods belonging to my husband.

Hereupon we drew up a binding agreement, protected with every safeguard. Judah then returned to Hildesheim and said he would bring together the money for which he was obligated, and in two or three weeks he would journey with my husband to Amsterdam. Meanwhile my husband put everything into shape and sent on his money to Amsterdam, and naught remained but for Judah to come with his. And come he did at the appointed time, but all he brought was bills of exchange for 500 thalers.

«What does this mean?» we said to him. «There should be two thousand thalers.» Whereupon he answered, «I have left a quantity of gold with my wife who will sell it off and forward me the balance from Hildesheim.» With this we were content.

So they set out together, and, in God's name, arrived safely in Amsterdam where, as the custom then was, my husband began by making small purchases. At every mail he asked Judah, «Has your money come?» And everytime Judah responded, «I'm getting it, I'll have it.» But nothing happened and nothing came.

What could my husband do? Judah gave him fair words and talked him over, so, together with Judah's 500 thalers my husband laid out all his money in wares as quickly as only one can in Amsterdam.

Then my husband returned here and Judah proceeded to Hildesheim. He took with him all my husband's purchases and travelled about to sell or barter them after his heart's desire.

Once home, my husband began to talk with me and grumble that I had persuaded him to enter the partnership. At the very outset, he said, Judah has not kept his bargain; what can one expect next, and where will it all end? In such a business you can, God forbid, break your neck.

I talked him out of his fears as best I knew how, and I told him no more than the truth. «Judah is a young man,» I said, «and what dowry did he get? Five hundred thalers. And he had eight or nine hundred more when he left us, and that's over two years ago. So how can he muster up two thousand? Nay, assume that he is penniless and we are sending him, as formerly, on a business trip and trusting him with thousands as we were wont to do—if God wills to bestow luck on a man, He can do so as well with little money as with much.»

What could my husband do? Whether he relished it or not, we were in for it and must smart for it. Thus some time went by and Judah, as he wrote us, made a bit of profit. But «a crumb will not satisfy a lion.»[17]

In short, the year was soon over and neither of us found it to our taste, for we saw that the profits were not enough to support even one household, much less two. So when the year's partnership came to an end, my husband journeyed to Hildesheim and cast up accounts with Judah. And he discovered, as I said, that neither of them could hold out in this fashion.

So he spoke to Judah like a brother, «You can plainly see that neither of us can go on with this partnership, that barely a thousand thalers has been earned altogether.» And Judah, in truth, saw it was so; and they dissolved the partnership of their own free will and in all friendship. My husband wrote out a dissolution paper for himself and another for Judah, and they both signed as customary.

Some thousands of thalers worth of rings and other jewellery remained on hand, which my husband turned over to Judah for him to sell and send us the proceeds. And a time was set for the payment of this money. But the time came and the money did not. So we wrote Judah a moderate and proper letter recalling to him his obligation and bidding him remit the money to Hamburg. Judah answered in a seemly fashion, he had not sold everything as yet, but purposed to remit the money as early as possible.

Finally, after more than a year had passed without receiving our money from Judah, my husband returned again to Hildesheim with the intention of getting it. Instead, he got something entirely different.

After Judah had kept my husband by him for several days, out it came, and he said to him, «I'll never give you a farthing and I'd like nothing better than to be holding from you twice as much as I do. Our partnership, according to the agreement, should have run ten years and it only ran for one. I'm entitled to thousands more from you, all that you have is mine, and even with it all you can't pay what you owe me.»

My husband was badly taken aback and said: «Judah, what kind of talk is this? Is this your thanks for all the kindness I have shown you? You came stark naked to my house and in a brief space I enabled you to take away nine hundred thalers cash. I have trusted you with thousands more, I have shown you every nook and corner where I thought you could do business, and because I took

you for an open and honest man I prevailed on my
brother Samuel to give you his daughter. What is
more, it is you who broke our agreement. Instead
of the two thousand thalers you were bound to put
into the concern, you put in only five hundred.
Besides, our agreement read that if the partnership
does not yield two thousand a year, it shall be dissolved. And in the end we saw it could not work.
So of our own free will we released ourselves and
duly signed the dissolution papers. What more now
do you want? I beg you, give folks no chance to
wag their tongues—after all, we are related and,
God willing, we can still do business together.» So
spake my husband, and more of the same order.
But it made no impression on my good man Judah;
he stuck to his song.

After many words and much wrangling, as is
customary in such matters, third parties intervened,
and shaking hands, my husband and Judah each
agreed to select an arbiter[18] and try the case before
the rabbi of Hildesheim, four months later. My
husband must consent to it all, for who can «contend with him that is mightier,»[19] and it is well
known that he who holds possession is the stronger.

My husband came home with these results and
told me the whole story. We were deeply afflicted
by it, for we knew we had dealt fairly and in truth
with the man and rendered him great kindnesses—
which God reward us! I was taken a little to task

because I had brought about the partnership, but God knows I did it for the best and had only meant to spare my husband the burden of travelling. I never dreamed it would end in this way, or expected the like of Judah, whom I had always held for an honest man.

That Judah may have suspected my husband of doing business unfitting for a partner or without his knowledge, I can never know. Perhaps the following transaction may have kindled the blaze:

When my husband first returned from Hildesheim, immediately after dissolving the partnership, he met in Hamburg a Frenchman stocked with various goods. They bartered together and my husband turned a nice profit. Now when a man makes a hundred thalers, Jews have a way of talking as if it were a thousand. Accordingly the rumour spread that my husband had garnered thousands, and coming right on the dissolution of the partnership Judah must have caught echo of it. So perhaps he imagined, or gave himself to believe, that my husband had this business already in view while the partnership was yet in force; and no doubt he was readier to believe it when people told him thousands had been made.

God knows the real truth of the matter! Never before had we perceived anything improper or unjust in the behaviour of the man. It was the sole time he turned upon us and refused to yield what he held in his hands. «Man looketh on the outward appearance, but the Lord looketh on the heart.»[20] Perhaps he thought he was right and stuck to his opinion. «No man can see his own guilt.»[21]

In any case Judah had his hands on a large sum of our money. And our peace was disturbed by it. I asked my husband why he allowed the suit to be brought before the court of Hildesheim, and told him he should have tried it in a neutral place. And he answered me in anger, «If you had been there, no doubt, you would have done better! The man holds my goods in his hands, and the thing must go as it suits him and not me.» But our quarrel ended, and we must contain ourselves in patience and leave all to God who had so often helped us in our need. We were young folks, just coming into our own, and now to tumble in this maze! We had to grope our way.

7

The Frankfort Fair was now about to open, and as usual my husband must travel there himself. He visited his brother in Frankfort, the learned Isaac Hameln, and related all that had come between him and Judah Berlin; and he begged his brother to recommend him a stout Talmud scholar, for he must presently appear in Hildesheim where, unless he chose to forego his claims, each party to the dispute must bring his own arbiter.

My brother-in-law Isaac at once said to my husband, «You have already lost your case, since you have consented to have it tried in your opponent's community.» My husband now repeated all his claims and difficulties, and my brother-in-law responded, «Brother mine, you are entirely in the right and your claims might well be upheld, had you unpartisan judges and pressed your suit in a neutral territory.» Whereat my husband said, «That can no longer be helped; the thing must now go as God wills and there is an end on't. Do but recommend me a good man.» After some reflection, my brother-in-law replied, «Reb Ascher who sits in our rabbinate has a young and good head. He will serve well enough, only—but I've said my say.»

My husband now went to Reb Ascher and showed him the agreement and the dissolution paper, whereupon Reb Ascher said, «Have no worry, your case is just and I will accompany you.»

During the fair my husband again consulted his brother as to whether he could recommend him an honest lad to serve in his business. In short, he recommended Issachar Cohen who was to play, alas, the Herod to my house, and of whom more will be told in its proper time and place.[22]

Once the fair was over, my husband and his arbiter journeyed to Hildesheim to plead their

suit. But how shall I write of it all? To relate everything that happened would fill a hundred sheets.
Our arbiter could make no progress, for he stood
alone with two against him. Nor would he allow
himself to be forced into agreement with an unjust decision. Threatened with imprisonment if he
would not yield, my good Reb Ascher secretly
slipped out of Hildesheim, but not before he had
written down and left behind him a long opinion
in favour of my husband.[23]

The rabbi of Hildesheim and a *parnas* of the
community—I will name no names, for all are now
in the Eternal Truth—stood body and soul behind
Judah Berlin and tried with all their might to force
on my husband a creditor's arrangement, but one
that would have borne hard on him. My husband
had no mind to accept these terms, and matters
were headed for an interminable suit in the civil
courts.

But my father-in-law, who was now living in
Hildesheim, begged my husband, truly with tears
in his eyes, «My dear son,» he said, «you see for
yourself what passes here; I pray you, for God's
sake, let not the matter run into endless litigation;
possess your soul in patience and make the best
terms you can. The good Lord will bless you again
with goods, and in greater plenty.»

So, against his will, my husband consented to an
arrangement. You can well imagine its terms. This

much I know, that when all was said and done, it cost us more than a third of everything we had.

I hold Judah Berlin in less blame than those who abetted him. But we have now forgiven all of them. Nor do we grumble over Judah nor hold ill will against him. He must have thought he was right and asking no more than his due; otherwise he would not—perhaps—have behaved as he did. Yet it went hard on my husband. But who could have helped him? «Who prays for what is past, prays in vain.»[24]

And the good Lord, who saw our innocence, bestowed on us, e'er four weeks had passed, such excellent business that we close repaired our losses. Later, too, my husband lived with Judah on terms of confidence and understanding. And I will in good time tell you of the honours Judah and his wife paid me when I was in Berlin. He never failed, either, to do a good business turn for my children, so all in all we could not complain of him.

I feel that had our partnership continued with good profits, nothing would have ever come between us. But our falling out, it seems, proved to be a happy stroke for Issachar Cohen. From then on his luck began to bloom.

8

The whole matter, like everything else in my book, is of no consequence and I have written it down merely to drive away the idle melancholy thoughts that torment me.

Yet you may see from it how all things here below change with the course of time. «God makes us ladders, and one man is given to mount and another to descend.»[25] Judah Berlin came to us with nothing; but, with God's help, he would not, I believe, sell out today for 100,000 Reichsthalers. Moreover, he has his hand in such business and enjoys such *Aestimation* from the Elector, God increase his glory! that in my opinion, if he continues his march and God be not against him, he will die the richest man in all Germany.

You may also see how many we have helped, with God's aid, to make their way, and how all who have done business for us have become wealthy, but most of them without gratitude, as is the way of the world.

Quite the contrary, many we rendered good have repaid us or our children with evil. But God Almighty is just; and we sinful creatures cannot tell, we do not even know, what is good or bad for us. Many a man, when things go contrary, thinks he is suffering evil, yet the very thing we hold an evil may prove a blessing. If faithful honest Mordecai, God revenge his death! had been spared, many of us would perhaps have escaped a drubbing and doubtless he would himself have become a big man.

We now took on Green Moses; in truth, we did

not do a great business with him, yet as I have
mentioned we made together a number of tidy
deals in seed pearls. He travelled afar, and left his
wife and children in Hamburg. We must needs
support them, even without knowing whether the
profits would cover us. It was a case of casting
bread upon the waters. To put it in brief, while
we did not profit overmuch, we managed nicely
to make both ends meet. We would gladly have
continued our dealings together had he not departed from Hamburg and settled in Schottland,
hard by Danzig. Things have not gone badly with
him there, and he prospers.

Abraham Cantor of Copenhagen, who served in
our house as a lad, did honestly and well by himself. Later, we sent him on a number of occasions
to Copenhagen. There he became rich and settled
afterwards with wife and children. I am told that
today he is a man worth 15,000 Reichsthalers and
enjoys his good business; he gives his children thousands for dowry.

My kinsman Mordecai Cohen and Loeb Bischere
entered into a partnership with my husband. He
provided them with money and letters of credit
and sent them on to England; but because of the
war they failed to reach their destination, and the
English trip was abandoned.[26] Nevertheless, they
placed a sum of money in Amsterdam against good
interest, whereupon my relative Mordecai Cohen

travelled through Holland and Brabant and turned very good profits. So this first trip of his laid the foundation of his business and fortune.

My brother-in-law Elias Ries was an inexperienced youth, skilled as yet in no business. My husband, however, advanced him large credits on the spot, and finally sent him with 20,000 Reichsthalers' credit to Amsterdam.

Many of our Hamburg people, pillars of the community today, have thanked God when we extended them credit. I would fain name more of them, but what good will it do? Where now is the kindness that you, my good and faithful Chayim Hameln, showered on all the world? Gladly gave you this one a helping hand and that one an open heart, and often despite your own distress and again to your own cost. There were times he knew full well no profit could come of it, and his deed was all of loving kindness. And so honourable today are your dear and pious children, that in the face of offence, be it the slightest, they would rather die than seek to harm another.

But of all who took our help, no one seemed to remember it. Yet well they could have given a bit of kindly aid to my dear children, young folks too soon bereft of their good father and lost like «sheep that have no shepherd.»[27]

God help us, it was just the contrary. They caused the loss of thousands to my children, and brought it to pass that the money of my son Mordecai fell into base hands. The president of the Council and the entire court agreed it was an honourable deal and that the merchants had no further claim for payment on their wares, for he had openly and honestly bought them. Yet they gave him no peace. On the eve of the Day of Atonement he was compelled to sign away his money and come to such terms with the merchants that, more than aught else, it brought on his ruin. May the great and good God take into account what that meant for him and for me, and let it be an atonement for our sins. They forced my son to it in the «name of God,»[28] and may God reward them according to their deeds.

I cannot accuse the man I have in mind for I am ignorant of his thoughts: «man looketh on the outward appearance, but the Lord looketh on the heart.» But this I know full well; my children were young and needed credit, as the rule of business goes; they proposed to sell certain bills of exchange, and merchants took the bills and told them to return after the Bourse was closed. I suspect that the one merchant, meanwhile, made inquiries of a certain Jew he held in high esteem. When my children returned to the merchant, after the Bourse was over, in order to receive cash for their good bills bearing good endorsements, the merchant handed them back the bills. In consequence, they often suffered thereafter for lack of credit.

Great and only God, I implore Thee from the depth of my heart to forgive me my thought. Truly I may have wronged the man I suspected, and well may it be that what he did was done in the «name of God.» We must give all into God's hands and remember that this vain world is not for long.

9

Thou knowest well, Almighty God, how I pass my days in trouble and affliction of heart. I was long a woman who stood high in the esteem of her pious husband, who was like the apple of his eye. But with his passing, passed away my treasure and my honour, which all my days and years I now lament and bemoan.

I know that this complaining and mourning is a weakness of mine and a grievous fault. Far better it would be if every day I fell upon my knees and thanked the Lord for the tender mercies He has bestowed on my unworthy self. I sit to this day and date at my own table, eat what I relish, stretch myself at night in my own bed, and have even a shilling to waste, so long as the good God pleases. I have my beloved children, and while things do not always go as well, now with one or the other, as they should, still we are all alive and acknowledge our Creator. How many people there are in this world, finer, better, juster and truer than I, such as I know myself for patterns of piety, who have not bread to put into their mouths! How, then, can I thank and praise my Creator enough for all the goodness He has lavished on us without requital!

If only we poor sinners would acknowledge the everlasting mercy of our God who from the dust of the ground formed us into men, and that we may serve our Creator with all our heart, gave us to know His great and terrible and holy Name!

Behold, my children, all a man will do to gain the favour of a king, flesh and blood that he is, here to-day and tomorrow in his grave, no one knowing how long may live he who asks or he who gives. And behold the gifts he receives from the transient hand of a king. Honours the king can grant him and put him too in the way of wealth; yet honours and money are but for a space and not for eternity. A man may hoard his honours and his gold until the very last, and then comes bitter Death to make all forgotten; and his honours and his gold are of no avail. Every man, he knows this well and yet he strives loyally to serve a mortal king to gain the passing reward.

How much more, then, should we strive day and night, when we come to serve in duty bound the King of kings who lives and rules forever! For He

it is whence come the favours we receive from
human kings, and He it is who gives these kings
their all and who puts it in their heart to honour
whomsoever His holy will decrees, for «the king's
heart is in the hand of the Lord.»[29] And the gifts
of a human monarch stand as naught against the
gift of the God of Glory upon those whom He
delights to honour: eternity without stain, measure
or term.

So, dear children of my heart, be comforted and
patient in your sorrows and serve the Almighty
God with all your hearts, in your evil days as in
your good; for although we often feel we must
sink beneath our heavy burdens, our great Lord and
Master, we must know, never lays upon His servants more than they can bear. Happy the man who
accepts in patience all that God ordains for him or
for his children.

Wherefore I, too, beg my Creator give me
strength to bear without fret the contrarieties of
the world, all of them, be it said, of our own making. «Man is bound to give thanks for the evil as
for the good.»[30] Let us commend all into the hands
of God, and I will now resume my tale.

10

My daughter Mata was now in her third year,
and never was there a lovelier and more charming
child. Not only we but everyone who lay eyes on

her or heard her prattle, delighted in the mite. But the Lord delighted in her more, and as she entered her third year, her hands and feet swelled of a sudden. Although we employed doctors and physicking of all sorts, still it pleased the good Lord, after the child had suffered four weeks in pain, to recall His share unto Himself and leave ours lying before us, to the breaking of our hearts.

My husband and I grieved beyond all telling, and I greatly fear I sinned in this before the Lord, and brought on myself a heavier punishment than, alas, I already deserved. Both of us mourned so bitterly that for a long while we lay grievously ill; and so we had our great sorrow.

I now became expectant with my daughter Hannah and was brought to bed. Because of my grief for my dear departed child, with whose loss I could not be reconciled, I fell dangerously ill. I continued stricken throughout the time I lay in childbed, and the doctors, doubting of my recovery, wanted to bring desperate measures into play.

When they proposed these measures and explained them to my people, little thinking I knew or understood what they said, I told my husband and my mother I would not submit to them. Whereat they informed the doctors of my decision, and although the physicians meant well and did their best to persuade me, all their talk proved useless and I said to them, «Talk as much as you please, I'll take no more of your physicking. If the dear Lord minds to help me, He can do very well without medicines. If not, what good are all the medicines in the world?» In sum, I begged my husband discharge and pay the doctors, one and all. And so he did.

God gave me, then, the strength I needed, and in five weeks after I came to bed, though still miserable, I was able to go to synagogue. And I praised and thanked my God for all He had done. Each day I grew a little better, and finally I dismissed my attendant and wet-nurse and with the help of the Most High resumed my household duties, and in the end managed to forget the loss of my dear child, as God meant it.

Rabbi Jochanan ben Zakkai[31] had ten sons; nine of them died during the course of his life, and in his old age he clung to the last, a little child of three. His household were preparing one day a large wash and set a big kettle of water on the fire. It bubbled and seethed, and there was a bench full of wash standing by the kettle. They set the child on the bench and gave him no further thought. And childlike he stood up and wanted to peep into the kettle. But the bench was shaky and suddenly the child pitched forward and into the boiling water. And he gave one cry, and everyone ran to him, and the father tried to save his child. But he drew forth only a finger. And he struck his head against the wall and he cried, «Weep for my unhappy stars, for only a bone remains me of my tenth sacrifice to the Lord.» And, without more ado, he hung the bone about his neck; when Talmud scholars from afar came to visit him, he quietly pointed to the bone as though he would show them his child.

Now Rabbi Jochanan was a mighty scholar; he mastered Talmud, Mishna and Torah, he understood Kabbala and the mystery of creation, he could summon angels and conjure away demons, he read the stars of the heavens and knew what the leaves of the trees were saying—and if such could befall the great and good Rabbi Jochanan, what shall happen to others? Yet he remained a patient pious man to the end of his days.

Thus we must ever keep a measure in our grief when, God help us! the evil days are come, and knowing that His judgment is just, glorify the true and righteous Judge.

All of us suffer bitter losses, but far from helping us, grief and mourning only harm our body and weaken our soul. And no one depressed in body can worship God as he should. When the prophets of old invited the spirit of the Lord to come on them, they played the tabret, pipe and harp to rejoice their limbs, for the spirit of the Lord is slow to come on the sick in body.

THE END OF MY THIRD BOOK

BOOK FOUR

1

MY DAUGHTER Hannah had now grown into a lovely child, and later I may tell more of her.

About this time, an East Indian ship laden with uncut diamonds fell into the hands of the king of Denmark and lay in Glückstadt. The crew had their pockets full of gems which the Jews hastened to buy and which they picked up at a nice profit.

Two of the Jews learned that a burgher living in Norway had come by a goodly share of the stones, a baker I think he was, who had paid little for them. So our two scoundrels laid a wicked plot against him, and took ship for Norway. Making inquiries, they quickly located the burgher, fostered an acquaintance with him and managed to become his lodgers for the night. They soon discovered the hiding-place of the treasure, and in the middle of the night laid hands on it. They fled from the house at dawn, and hiring a small boat fancied they had brought the matter to a happy conclusion.

But God Almighty willed otherwise. Early in the morning the burgher arose and inquired after his guests. The servant told him they had left at the crack of dawn. Day and night the burgher naturally had a mind for nothing but his treasure, so he ran to the chest where he kept it, and found it empty. He at once suspected his guests of foul play. Dashing to the harbour he asked the skippers if they had seen two Jews taking ship for sea. Whereupon they told him, Skipper So-and-so set forth with them an hour ago.

He lost no time in hiring a boat with four oarsmen, and in a short while he caught sight of the craft making off with the two thieves. They saw they were pursued, so they went and threw the whole treasure into the sea. The burgher soon overhauled them, and despite their clamour, forced them to return with him. «Take heed,» they cried, «to what you are doing! We are honest men and nothing of yours will be found on us, and you may be sure we'll know how to avenge this outrage.» For they had cast the treasure overboard in order, as they thought, to better their lies.

But it says in the Ten Commandments, «Thou shalt not steal.» Therefore the Lord, blessed be He, did not aid them, and they were brought back to the harbour. While they were stripped bare and thoroughly searched they persisted in their lies. But it proved of no avail. They were then racked with tortures until they confessed what they had done and how, observing they were pursued, they had thrown the treasure into the sea.

They had thought that once they were searched and nothing found, they could brazen it out with lies. But, as we said, God willed otherwise. And both of them were now condemned to the gallows.

One of the thieves immediately embraced the Christian religion to avoid the death penalty. But the other, an observant Jew all his days and of pious parents—he came from Wandsbeck—would not renounce his faith, but chose rather to lose his life. I knew both him and his parents well; he had always conducted himself as a pious and upright man. He was doubtless led astray by his mate, of whom, his whole life long, nothing good was ever known. And so he needs must come to this unhappy end. Surely his soul is now in Paradise and in his last hour he earned his portion in the world to come. For his family's sake, I will not name him, although the whole story is well known in Hamburg. Of a surety God has accepted the sacrifice of his life in the sanctification of the Holy Name, for he could have saved himself as readily as his comrade. Instead, he obeyed the commandment, «Love thy God with all thy soul» and his death must have atoned for all his sins.

We should learn from this not to be misled by the love of worldly goods. For it is not enough to serve God with all our soul; the commandment adds «and with all thy might,» meaning with all our possessions. . . .

2

But to return to my subject. I came to bed with my son Mordecai, God grant his last day be as happy as his first. However, wish as we may, the Most High has already decreed whatever shall come to pass.

I mentioned in my third book our hope of redemption and that my father-in-law had sent us two casks in the expectation of proceeding with them to the Holy Land, when all Israel should be gathered there. When he saw that nothing came of it, he left Hameln and settled in Hildesheim, a pleasant and pious community only twenty-five miles from Hameln.

After they were settled there some little time, my husband, who loved his parents dearly and held them in high honour, said to me, «Glückelchen mine, let us go to Hildesheim and visit my father and mother; you have not seen them these twelve years.» I was content, so we took our maid and manservant and three of our children and we journeyed to Hildesheim.

I was still nursing my son Mordecai, who was not a year old. The servant, Samuel, was a handsome lad, and we used to call him Elegant Sam, for we once had another servant whom the children dubbed Clumsy Sam.

So we came to Hildesheim. My blessed parents-in-law had great joy in us, for my husband was their youngest child and things were then, God be praised, going well with us.

We brought with us what we felt sure would prove in Hildesheim a handsome and impressive gift. After spending three happy weeks together, we returned home safe and sound.

My father-in-law gave us, on our departure, a small tankard worth perhaps twenty Reichsthalers, but as dear to us as though it were worth a hundred. At that time, you must know, my father-in-law was a wealthy man, possessed of more than 20,000 Reichsthalers, and had all his children married. And our journey had cost us over 150 thalers. Yet we were as pleased as we could be with the twenty-thaler tankard, not like children are today, who want all they can get from their parents, stripping them to the bone, without considering whether or not they can afford it.

So we came home and found our other children in good health.

My father-in-law continued to live for some while in Hildesheim. But in four or five years he found it had cost him nearly 10,000 Reichsthalers. Although he kept a modest house, still the expenses were great, and the good folks saw that no purpose lay in remaining there. So they moved into the home of my rich brother-in-law, Leffmann Behrens, in Hanover, and there they died at a ripe old age and with a good name—but more of this at another time.

3

Our business prospered. And Zipporah, my eldest child, was now a girl of almost twelve. Whereat Loeb Hamburger in Amsterdam, the son of Reb Amschel, proposed her marriage to Kossmann, the son of Elias Cleve,[1] of blessed memory.

My husband was accustomed to travel to Amsterdam twice a year, and now, after writing the marriage broker he was coming to see what could be done, he set forth six weeks in advance of his usual time. The country was at war[2] and Elias Cleve had left his home in Cleves and moved with his people to Amsterdam.

As soon as my husband reached Amsterdam, rumours spread through Hamburg that the match had been arranged. It was mail-day when people read their letters at the Bourse. Many refused to believe the rumours, and betting ran high around the Bourse; some said one thing, others said another, as to whether the marriage would take place. For Elias Cleve was a great prince in Israel, he had the name of a man worth at least 100,000 Reichsthalers, and the name did not belie him. Whereas my hus-

band was still young, our fortunes had only begun
to rise, and our little home swarmed with children
—God be with them! But whatever the Most High
decrees must come to pass, whether we mortals
like it or not; and forty days before the birth of
every child, a call goes forth in Heaven: «Such-
and-such a child. shall be given the daughter of
So-and-so.»[3]

Well, my blessed husband concluded the match
with the rich Elias Cleve and settled on our
daughter a dowry of 2200 Reichsthalers in Dutch
money. They fixed the wedding for a year and a
half later in Cleves. My husband likewise undertook
to contribute 100 Reichsthalers towards the wedding expenses.

When time for the marriage drew near, I with a
babe at my breast, my husband, my daughter Zipporah the bride, our Rabbi Meir, who is now the
rabbi of Friedberg, a maidservant and our man
Elegant Sam—in sum, a great retinue—set forth
for the wedding.

We sailed from Altona in company with Mordecai Cohen, Meir Ilius and Aaron Todelche. I cannot begin to tell what a merry voyage it was. And
after a gay and delightful trip we arrived safely
in Amsterdam.

It was still three weeks before the wedding, and
we put up with the aforesaid Loeb Hamburger. We
ran through more than twelve ducats a week, but

BETROTHAL CEREMONY
A Vase Is Broken to Solemnize Signing of the Contract

we gave no thought to it, for during the time we passed in Amsterdam my husband earned a half of the dowry.

Fourteen days before the marriage we set forth «with timbrels and with dances,» twenty strong, for Cleves, where we were welcomed with all honours. We found ourselves in a house that was truly a king's palace, magnificently furnished in every way. The livelong day we had no rest for the elegant lords and ladies who came to have a peep at the bride. And in truth, my daughter looked so beautiful that her like was never seen.

Then came the great preparations for the wedding. At that time, Prince Frederick was in Cleves.[4] His older brother, Prince Elector Karl, still lived, and Prince Frederick was then a young lord about thirteen years of age. Not long after, Karl died and Frederick in turn became Prince Elector. Prince Maurice of Nassau and other titled personages and great lords were likewise in Cleves, and they all signified their desire to witness the nuptials.

Naturally, Elias Cleve, the father of the groom, made fitting preparations for such notable guests. On the marriage day, immediately after the wedding, there was spread a lavish collation of all kinds of sweetmeats and fine imported wines and fruits. You can readily picture the bustle and excitement, and how Elias Cleve and his people set themselves to wait upon and cater to their distinguished company. There was not even time to deliver and count over the dowries, as is customary. So we placed our own dowry in a pouch and sealed it, and Elias Cleve did likewise, that we might tally the sum after the wedding was over.

As the bridal pair were led beneath the *chuppah* [wedding canopy] out it came that in the confusion we had forgotten to write the marriage contract! What was to be done? Nobility and princes were already at hand and they were all agog to see the ceremony. Whereat Rabbi Meir declared that the groom should appoint a bondsman to write out the contract immediately after the wedding. Then the rabbi read a set-contract from a book. And so the couple were joined.

After the ceremony, all the distinguished guests were ushered into Elias Cleve's enormous salon with its walls of leather tooled in gold. There stood the mighty table laden with dainties fit for a king. And the company were served according to their rank.

My son Mordecai was then a child of about five; there was not a prettier boy in all the world, and we had him dressed in his neatest and best. All the nobility wanted to eat him up on the spot, and the Prince in particular, God heighten his fame! never let go his hand.

When the guests of honour had eaten of the fruit and cakes and had done justice to the wine, the table was cleared and removed. Then appeared masked performers who bowed prettily and played all manner of entertaining pranks. They concluded their performance with a truly splendid Dance of Death.[5]

A number of prominent Sephardim likewise attended the wedding, among them one Mocatta, a jeweller, who wore a beautiful small gold watch set with diamonds and worth no less than 500 Reichsthalers. Elias Cleve wanted to buy the little watch from Mocatta for a gift to the Prince. But a good friend who was standing by said to him, «What for?—why give the young Prince such a costly present? If, to be sure, he were already Prince Elector, well and good.» But, as I have said, the Prince Elector died soon after, and our young prince succeeded to the title and now he is Elector himself. And after that, every time Elias Cleve met his prudent friend he cast it in his teeth. In truth, if Elias Cleve had given the little watch, the young Prince would have always remembered it, for great lords never forget such things. But there is no point in grumbling over what is past.

As it was, the young Prince and Prince Maurice and all the noble-born guests departed in great content, and never a Jew received such high honour in a hundred years. And the wedding was brought to a happy end.

4

After the wedding I went to visit the grave of my sister Hendel, nearby in Emmerich. God alone knows the heartache and grief her death meant to me, and the pity of it—still—that one so young and more than fair must bite the black of earth. She was not twenty-five years old. But what good does it do? We must all yield to the will of God. She left behind her a son and a daughter. The son grew up to be a likely young man and an excellent Talmud student; but, alas, he died young and unmarried, mourned by all far and near.

The day following the wedding we set out in good spirits on our homeward journey. We passed through Amsterdam in order to retrace our steps, as it is written: «And he went on his journeys unto the place where his tent had been at the beginning.»[6] So we returned to Amsterdam, where we remained for about two weeks that my husband might do a little business.

Then we sailed for Delfzijl, which is reached by crossing the Dollart, a rough body of water where the ships roll so heavily that even the strongest man, if he be not used to the sea, falls deathly sick.

When we boarded ship we left our servants and children in the main cabin, which was as big as a house, and my husband and I hired from the skipper a small room where we could be alone. It had a sort of porthole which opened and closed at will, and you could look through it into the main cabin and hand things back and forth.

We entered our little room where we found two benches which served for lying down. My husband now said to me, «Glückelchen, stretch yourself nicely on a bench, and I will cover you warm and snug. Take good care not to stir, only lie still and the sea will not disturb you.» I had never crossed the Dollart, but my husband had time and again, and he knew what to do.

I did as he told me and lay quite still. The weather was bad, the winds were contrary, and the ship tossed so that everyone on board turned deathly sick and—pardon the expression—puked. There is truly no sickness like it in the whole world; I do believe the throes of death cannot be worse. However, as long as I lay still I felt nothing.

But my maid, who had my baby with her in the main cabin, fell sick and could not lift her hand, and the baby, no doubt, felt none too well and began to scream and howl. The maid was unable to stir and had to let the baby go on crying. A mother pitying her child, I could hold back no longer. I rose from my place and drew the baby to me through the porthole, and laid it to my breast.

God, how I fell sick—as though I were suddenly thrust at death's door! I thought my end had come and I began to recite the confession for our sins as well as I could and as much as I remembered by heart. My husband continued to lie quietly on his bench, knowing well it was no mortal illness, and that once I put foot on dry land it would pass. When he heard me confess my sins and turn my thoughts to God, he began to laugh. I heard him and I thought to myself, «Here I am at death's door, and my husband lies there and laughs.» Although I was mighty angry, still this was not the time to quarrel with your husband; moreover I hadn't the strength to say a word. So I had to remain lying in my agony until, in about a half an hour, we touched land and left the ship. And our sickness, God be praised, vanished at once.

Night had fallen when we landed at Delfzijl, and it was too late to find lodging in an inn or even a Jew's house. It was still storming and we feared nothing remained for us but to spend the night in the street. The following day was the fast before the New Year, and we had not eaten a bite all day on shipboard, and we were still faint from our seasickness. So we did not relish lying in the street all night without food or drink.

But presently my husband came to the house of a Jew whose brother had married the daughter of Chayim Fürst of Hamburg, and begged a night's shelter for us and our children, so at least we should have a roof over our heads. The man of the house immediately said, «Enter, in God's name, my house is yours—I can give you a good bed but food there is none»; for it was already late and his wife was away in Emden.

My husband was delighted at finding even shelter and he brought us to the house without delay. We still had with us a morsel of bread which we gave to the children. As for myself, I thanked God I had a bed, and a good bed it was, better than food or drink.

5

We rose early next morning and sailed to Emden where we were guests of Abraham Stadthagen— his father, Moses Kramer of Stadthagen, was my husband's uncle. We passed the New Year in Emden, and so pleasantly we quite forgot the Dollart.

Abraham Stadthagen had a heart of gold. Not only did he entertain us handsomely and show us all the honours in the world, but he had at table six penniless strangers sent him by the community, and they partook of the same food and drink as we —something I've yet to see at the table of a rich man.

We left Emden upon the close of the New Year festival, thinking to arrive home by the Day of Atonement. Early in the morning we reached Wittmund where we engaged passage for Hamburg. Now, a day's journey brings you to Wangeroog where ships put in to pay customs and take on supplies.

When we reached Wangeroog, the local authority asked us our destination, and my husband said, «We are going to Hamburg.» Whereupon he said, «I warn you, you will never arrive—for the sea is filled with privateers which make off with everything they can.»

We had already paid our ten thalers for the passage, and the Day of Atonement was drawing near; nevertheless, we had to abandon our voyage and betake ourselves again to Wittmund. There we agreed to pass the holy day as guests of Breinle, my husband's cousin.

We consulted with her as to how we might proceed. Privateers barred the way by sea, and wherever you turned soldiers overran the land. So we sought advice from the people of Wittmund.

The widow Breinle came from Hamburg, the daughter of Loeb Altona, an altogether wise and devout woman; moreover, she was a near kin of my husband and ever our good friend. Accordingly, she did all in her power to help us onward.

At length it was decided that once the holy days were over, we would travel home by land. Meanwhile my husband should go to Aurich where he was to secure a passport from General Buditz who, we were told, had served under various dukes and monarchs; he was everywhere held in high esteem and a pass from him would carry us through all lines. To make doubly sure, Meir Aurich was to prevail on General Buditz to grant us a stout officer as a *salvaguardia* on our way.

My husband set forth for Aurich the day before Yom Kippur and returned just as we sat down to eat the last meal before the fast. He had secured everything we desired, even to bringing back a corporal, a valiant and honest soul, who accompanied us to Hamburg.

Immediately after the Day of Atonement we hired coach for Oldenburg. It came to nigh as much as buying the coach and horses outright; otherwise, every driver stood in such fear for his mount, none would run the risk.

You may imagine my husband's distress and his state of nerves. As for myself, I had to take off my good travelling clothes and dress myself in rags.

Our Rabbi Meir, who was accompanying us, said to my husband, «My good Reb Chayim, why this ill humour and why clad your wife so hideously?» Whereat my husband answered, «God knows I care naught for myself nor my money either; I am worried only for our womenfolk, my wife and maid.» «You needn't worry over them,» said Rabbi Meir; «in fact, you quite deceive yourself with regard to your wife. She needn't get herself up so abominably, no one would touch her anyway.» And my husband fell into a fury with

Rabbi Meir for showing his wit at a moment when he was himself distraught with worry.

We left Wittmund towards midnight, and Breinle and all the good people of Wittmund accompanied us a fair piece of the way, showering on us their dearest blessings. So we came safely to Oldenburg.

Need I write of all that befell us in Bremervörde and elsewhere? Enough that with the help of God, the faithful corporal, and the good passport we made our way.

When we reached Oldenburg we found the whole place swarming with soldiers, and the driver we had hired in Wittmund refused to carry us farther, even if we gave him all the money in the world. Whereat my husband must run everywhere in search of another coach. At last he found one at a steep price in a village ten miles away. So we set out for the village, and towards nightfall arrived there without mishap.

That evening we were sitting by the fire, and our host and other villagers had gathered about us, smoking tobacco. The talk turned on this place and that, and a peasant began speaking of the Duke of Hanover. «My lord and master,» he said, «has likewise sent twelve thousand men into Holland.»[7] Whereat my husband rejoiced mightily to learn that he was now on Hanoverian soil. For the Lüne-

Family Celebration of the Feast of Booths

burg dukes keep order in their land; a soldier dare not so much as ruffle the feather of a hen.

My husband at once asked the distance to Hanover. The peasant told him, forty miles; and together they reckoned that by setting forth next day we could reach Hanover before the Feast of Booths. My husband hired coach on the spot, and next evening we continued our journey.

It gave my husband great joy to have things so fall out that, together with his wife and children, he could fulfill the commandment, «Honour thy father and mother,» by passing the holy days with his dear parents. And after all our unwonted troubles and worries we arrived happily in Hanover.

My father-in-law came to meet us beyond the city gate—like an angel, like the Prophet Elijah himself—with his staff in his hand, his ruddy cheeks and his snowy beard falling to his girdle. Truly, if an artist sought to paint a handsome old man he could not have done better. How our hearts quickened at the sight of him and the joy we lived through that first day of the feast can never be told.

However, during mid-festival we left straightway for Hamburg. My parents-in-law would gladly have had us remain over the holidays, but our circumstances did not permit of it and we managed to explain to them our reasons. So we departed

from them in good spirits, and, alas, I never in this
world saw either of them again. God grant me the
grace, when He calls me from our world of sin,
to place me at their side in Paradise!

Though we would have willingly discharged our
corporal and paid him well, he begged of us to take
him to Hamburg. He had heard so much of it and
never had been there in all his life. Because of his
decent behaviour throughout the journey, my husband hadn't the heart to deny him, and we took
him with us.

We arrived betimes, on the day before the close
of the festival, and God be praised and thanked,
found all our family in good health. The entire
journey, to and fro, cost us over 400 Reichsthalers.
But we did not weigh the price, for our business,
thank God, was prosperous. God be praised He
has not withheld His ever-faithful love, but has
abode with us to this hour!

After many pains we were in our own home
again.

6

A certain Reb Moses lived for some while in
Helmstädt, a town, as I recall it, about twenty-five
miles from Hildesheim. It was the seat of a univer-
sity and hence a bad place for Jews.[8] So Reb Moses
was expelled from Helmstädt and betook himself

to Pomerania, where he managed to secure the right
to reside in Stettin.

There he procured himself powerful letters of
protection, and likewise the mint patent, so that he
alone had the right in Stettin to coin money. The
patent fixed the fineness of the coins and their pur-
chase price, and the government appointed a commissioner to oversee the mintage.

But Moses Helmstädt hadn't enough money of
his own to carry out this big undertaking. So he
wrote my husband, enclosing his letters of protection and asking my husband if he wished to furnish
the silver; if so, he might have a share of the coinage and of whatever jewels were bought or sold.

Stettin was an important city. It was well a
hundred years or more since a Jew had lived there,
but great numbers of Jews often visited the place,
to buy up pearls and precious stones at low prices.
Precious stones could also be sold there to good
advantage.

Moreover, my husband reckoned that a tidy
profit lay in the *Drittel* [a coin worth one-third
thaler]; 100,000 Stettin *Drittel* could readily be
exchanged for almost as good as new *Drittel* of
Lüneburg and Brandenburg. So my husband wrote
Reb Moses that if he meant honestly by his proposal he was prepared to enter into the partnership.

Previous to settling in Stettin, Reb Moses had
lived for a number of years in Berlin where he left

a load of debts behind him—of which, alas, we knew nothing. We knew indeed he was not a man of means; we only marked that he had fixed himself in an important city, come by excellent letters of protection, and that, further, the whole land lay open before him and that he and ten like him could have made their way to wealth and greatness. We never learned of his debts till later, and then to our great damage, as the sequel will show.

We sent to Stettin my son Nathan, then a lad of about fifteen, somewhat to keep an eye on things. We now began to ship Moses Helmstädt large quantities of silver which he delivered to the mint; and in return he sent us Stettin *Drittel* which we immediately sold on the Bourse. The transaction yielded us a nice profit, at times two per cent or more, and again somewhat less, following the rate of exchange. We also received from him sundry consignments of pearls which likewise brought a good profit, and we were well content.

7

A year or so previously, I had come to bed with my daughter Esther.

At that time a number of matches were proposed for my son Nathan, among them the bereaved daughter of the rich *parnas* of the community, Elijah Ballin of blessed memory. On the other hand, a match was proposed with the daughter of the wealthy Samuel Oppenheimer[9] and fell little short of being clinched. But it seemed as though God had decreed nothing should come of it.

We parents were both to send our dowries to my brother-in-law Isaac Hameln, in Frankfort. So we deposited with him precious stones worth several thousands, and Samuel Oppenheimer likewise sent on his dowry. But winter and floods delayed the delivery of his money fourteen days beyond the time agreed upon.

Meanwhile, the marriage broker pressed upon us the match with Elijah Ballin's daughter. My husband said to himself, «My brother Isaac does not write me that the money has reached Frankfort in accordance with the agreement. No doubt the rich Samuel Oppenheimer has changed his mind, and if we dally over the match with Elijah Ballin's daughter, we shall find ourselves tumbling between two stools.»

So we resolved to give our blessing to the Ballin match. The mother of the fatherless child engaged herself to the amount of 4000 Reichsthalers *banko*, in addition to the wedding expenses; and we in turn to give our son Nathan 2400 Reichsthalers *banko*. Thereupon the betrothal stood fast.

Eight days later came a letter from my brother-in-law Isaac; the money had arrived, and my husband should without delay send on the authorization to conclude the match. But it was too late.

My husband sent his apologies to his brother: he
had thought that fourteen days having elapsed beyond the agreed limit, Samuel Oppenheimer had
turned his mind elsewhere, and as for himself, having received another offer to his liking, he had felt
obliged in the doubtful circumstances to accept it;
he hoped, in conclusion, that Samuel Oppenheimer
might likewise find a match to his content.

Good Lord, the furious answer this letter
whipped from my brother-in-law Isaac! I dare not
repeat it. But things over and done are not to be
changed.

We were, moreover, content with our bargain—
altogether a notable match. The departed Elijah
Ballin was a good and just man, held in high regard among both Jews and Gentiles, for many years
before his death he was *parnas* of our community,
and 4000 thalers *banko* was no mean dowry.

If God had prospered the young couple so they
could have arisen like the rich prince Samuel Op-
penheim, who the longer he lives the higher he
goes, all would have been well. But the great and
merciful God bestows His gifts and tenderness as
He pleases. Without questioning His ways, we ignorant mortals must in all things thank our
Creator.

Upon his betrothal, we brought my son Nathan
back home, that he make his gift to the bride. This
too was celebrated with high feasting, and the be-

CONTEMPORARY PORTRAIT OF SAMUEL OPPENHEIMER

trothal began, praise God, with great joy on both sides.

Two weeks later my son returned to Stettin.

8

We continued our business with Moses Helmstädt. But he was a faithless man, and such as he, when once they fall into money, whether it belongs to them or not, so long as they have it in hand, cannot restrain themselves from calling it their own—as we learned, God have mercy, to our cost.

The trouble began when he laid to the commissioner or cashier an error amounting to a thousand thalers. The latter refused to concede the mistake and insisted he was in the right, whereupon Moses Helmstädt set out to sue him in the Stettin courts —which cost a tidy sum of money.

And then he showed himself for what he was— a bold-faced, arrogant, impudent and downright scoundrel. He never had less than 10,000 to 12,000 Reichsthalers *banko* in his hands, and he never once considered, as it behooved an honest man, that the money was not his, or that he needs must one day repay it to his creditor.

His thoughts turned on nothing but the money that lay before his eyes and the joy he could take in spending it while he had it. He bought himself a magnificent *calèche* and a pair of the best horses

to be had in Stettin, got himself two or three
flunkeys and maidservants, and lived like a prince.
Yet the profits from his business were never very
great.

Before coming to Stettin, he had lived, as I remarked, in Berlin, whence he was compelled to depart because of his debts and double-dealing. And
now that the puffed-up fool found his hands filled
with the money of our good Chayim Hameln, he
could hold in no longer, and he, no doubt, said to
himself, «I'll show those rascals in Berlin the kind
of man that I've become.»

So he takes his *calèche* and four horses, and some
2000 or 3000 thalers in *Drittel*, and he writes us
that he intends to exchange the *Drittel* for ducats
in Berlin, and later send us the ducats by post. In
itself this was not an uncommon procedure; a
gain of one per cent lay in the exchange, and, moreover, the cost of shipping ducats came to less than
shipping *Drittel*. This, then, was all very well.

But when my good Moses Helmstädt arrived in
Berlin, he began to clink his money about, for folly
and money are bound to make a noise. His creditors, Jews and Gentiles, had good ears and they
clapped our Reb Moses in jail. In short, he found
no means of leaving the city until he had paid out
1800 Reichsthalers—of Chayim Hameln's money.

He returned to Stettin, but he sent neither ducats nor *Drittel* to the good Chayim Hameln. Up

to date he had from us more than 12,000 Reichsthalers *banko*.

At length we received 2000 Reichsthalers, and he
wrote us to send him further shipments of silver,
lest the mint stand idle.

Although my son Nathan misliked the whole
business, he dared not write us, for all his letters
were opened. He finally slipped us word through
certain merchants, urging my husband to hasten
at once to Stettin.

Issachar Cohen, it happened, had just returned
from Courland. Though I ought to have told the
whole story of this Issachar pages ago, for he was
already with us more than ten years, I will postpone
it for another time, especially a full picture of the
man himself. Whether now or later is of no consequence.

Anyway, my husband said to Issachar Cohen,
«You must go with me to Stettin, and we must see
how matters stand.» So they went together to
Stettin and sought to cast up accounts with Moses
Helmstädt.

But he put them off from one day to another,
and gave my husband a bit of gold and pearls and
sundry bills of exchange on Hamburg. Finally my
husband would stand delay no longer, and Moses
Helmstädt needs must show his accounts. By his
own reckoning they were 5500 Reichsthalers short.

You may imagine my husband's distress and how his face fell.

Whereat Moses Helmstädt said to him, «Brother, I plainly see you are displeased with the accounts, and I cannot blame you. My mistake has been to tie up your money. But do not worry. I will sign you notes for it, and in less than a year and six months you will be repaid in full. Come now with me to the room where I pray.»

He led my husband upstairs to a little *Betstube* [oratory] he had in his house. He drew the holy scrolls of the Law from their holy shrine and held them in his arm. And he swore by every holy letter in scrolls and by what I dare not write in vain,[10] he would pay his every note as they fell due.

He had, he swore, the means to pay, his money was merely tied up; and once paid, my husband would find himself so well satisfied he would be happy to continue their business together. He continued in this strain a flow of words not worth the paper it would take to repeat them.

Although my husband was mightily displeased and Issachar Cohen swelled with wrath and wanted to resort to force and sue the delinquent, still my husband saw no point in bringing suit before the Stettin courts, for Sweden was an evil land.[11]

Downcast, my husband returned home with his notes, and brought me the painful tidings. He would have preferred not to tell me the like of it, but all his life he kept back nothing from me.

At the time, I was big with my son Loeb. And you can picture our distress. Not two weeks before, we had lost 1500 thalers through a bankruptcy in Prague and another 1000 thalers through a merchant in Hamburg. My son Nathan was engaged to boot, and would be married in something like six months, and that cost us over 3000 Reichsthalers. In short, we reckoned that the year had lost us more than 11,000 Reichsthalers *banko*.

With it all, we were still, so to say, in our youth, we had married off our eldest child, and we had our little home filled with children, God be with them. And now we were hard put to hold up our good name, and we had to bear it all in silence.

I fell downright sick from worry, though in the eyes of the world I blamed my illness on my pregnancy. But «a fire burned my entrails.» And my husband and I consoled each other as best we could.

The Frankfort Fair was now at hand, and as usual my husband must make the journey himself. He had arrived from Stettin on a Thursday morning and the next day saw him leave for Frankfort. It was with a heavy heart he left me.

Before he set forth, I had begged Issachar Cohen in Heaven's name go with him; for he was so disheartened, it misliked me to see him travel alone. But with his usual malice, Issachar Cohen refused to accompany him until my husband promised him two per cent of all he bought or sold. What else could be done? I did not wish my husband to set forth by himself, so we had to yield to Issachar's demands.

My husband exhorted and besought me to think no more on our misfortune. I had to give him my hand that I would forget it, and in return my husband promised me as much. We received little enough, I might tell you, from Moses Helmstädt's notes. Of all our money, not more than one note was paid; as for the rest, he disowned his signature and the matter cost us several hundreds more.

My husband reached Harburg on Friday and remained there over the Sabbath, till the departure of the post on Saturday night. He managed to write me from Harburg a long consoling letter. I should calm my aching heart, God would retrieve us our fortunes elsewhere.

And so it proved. My husband did more business at the Frankfort Fair than ever before in his life; the profits ran into the thousands, wherefore, thanks be to the Most High who withdrew not from us His mercy and grace, and who hath ever sent a healing for every wound!

At that very hour I had thought myself more afflicted and bowed down than anyone else in the world. I had quite forgotten the old saying:

Die ganze Welt ist voll Pein,
Ein jeder find't das Sein.

(The world is one long groan,
Which each man calls his own.)

A philosopher was once walking along the street, and meeting an old friend, asked him how things were going. Thanking him, the friend replied, «Badly. No one in the world has more sorrows and troubles than I.» Whereupon the philosopher said, «Good friend, come with me to my roof-top. I will point you every house in the whole city, and tell you the misfortunes and miseries they one and all conceal. Then, if you will, you may cast your own sorrow in with the rest and draw out any other you choose in its stead. Perhaps you will find one more to your liking.»

Together they climbed to the roof, and the philosopher showed his friend the unhappiness that darkened one house after the other. And he said, «Do now as I told you.» But the friend replied, «In truth, I see that every house hides as much woe and hardship as my own, and perhaps more. I think I'll keep what I have.»

So run the thoughts of men: each thinks his own burden to be the heaviest. Wherefore naught is better than patience. For if it pleases God Almighty, He can lift our burden in a trice.

9

Now it was that my father fell grievously ill. He had long suffered from the gout, but this proved to be fatal. His limbs began to swell and for more than three months he lay on his sick-bed. We were with him every evening, often till midnight, and time and again we thought his end had come.

As the hour grew nigh when God willed to take him from this passing world to life eternal, we sat with him far into the night. But since I was near to bearing my child, my mother induced me to return home with my husband.

When we had been in bed about an hour, some one from my father's house knocked on our door and bade my husband return at once. This had happened frequently, and we were not unused to it. My husband, therefore, would not suffer my accompanying him. He persuaded me to remain abed by promising to send for me, should the need arise. I allowed myself to be won over, and soon fell fast asleep.

My husband reached the house at the very moment my father had taken leave of the world. It was about midnight. My husband would not permit my being roused; two or three hours later, he said, would be time enough.

But as I lay sound asleep, three knocks resounded on my door, as though the whole house were tumbling in. I sprang from my bed and asked who knocked, but there came no word nor answer. I threw a dress about me and hastened to my father's house where I found all had come to pass as I have said.

You can well imagine my anguish, and how all of us grieved together. But what did it avail us? I needs must lose my beloved father. Dying at a ripe old age and with a good name, he forsook this life and all the living on the 24th of Tebet.

I found, in truth, no peace until, after the thirty days of mourning, I was blessed with a baby boy, through whom Loeb, my father's name, was born again.

But his birth seemed ill-omened. No sooner come into this world of woe, he lay and groaned for four-and-twenty hours. The midwife and all the womenfolk agreed he could never live it through. But it pleased the good Lord that the babe should pick up daily and grow to be a lovely child, a comfort in my father's stead; and I rejoiced in my son.

10

My beloved mother was left with three orphaned children. My father, of blessed memory, had bequeathed 1600 Reichsthalers to my mother and about 1400 Reichsthalers to each child. The children really should have had more, but they were despoiled of over a thousand thalers—wherefore I may write further.

My husband and Reb Joseph, my sister Elkele's husband, received nothing, although each of them had rightful claim to half the share of a son. But they renounced everything in favour of my mother and her bereaved children.

They likewise managed to betroth my brother Wolf, a year after my father's death, to the daughter of Jacob Lichtenstadt of Prague. Known as a good and just man, Reb Jacob presided as *parnas* of the province until his death, and he possessed enormous riches. But finally he came to strife with his stepson Abraham Lichtenstadt, so that toward the close of his life he was shorn of his wealth.

My brother-in-law Joseph accompanied my brother Wolf to the betrothal feast. On his return he told marvellous things of the elegance that reigned there and the splendour of the celebration. For Jacob Lichtenstadt's fortune was then at its height.

At the time of the next Leipzig Fair my husband escorted the bridegroom to the wedding itself, in company with Issachar Cohen who was still working for us. It was celebrated with all honours. Then my husband returned home, while my brother with his young wife remained on for some while.

Both my brother-in-law and my husband made

these journeys entirely at their own expense and never asked a penny for them from my mother.

As my father had placed all his estate in jewellery, so my husband and my brother-in-law bestirred themselves to arrange an auction. And they turned everything into cash, that my mother might give away her daughters, should a favourable match present itself.

Presently she betrothed my sister Mata, at the Leipzig Fair, to the son of the rich and learned Rabbi Model Ries;[12] and the wedding took place at Hamburg.

Everyone knows what an excellent man the Rabbi Model was, and Pessele, his pious wife, had not her like for goodness in the wide world. Such piety was never seen among women since the days of our mothers Sarah, Rebecca, Rachel and Leah. With it all, she was a mighty capable woman, she managed the business and amply provided for her husband and children, both in Vienna and when they later lived in Berlin.

For Rabbi Ries was a bedridden man, not able to attend to overmuch business. Yet he was a man of such pre-eminent wisdom, the whole world rang with his fame. He was likewise greatly beloved of the Elector of Brandenburg, God heighten his name! who once said of him, «If his legs were as good as his head, he would stand without rival.»

Both of them died at Berlin, in riches and honour. Her last will and testament makes remarkable reading. I would rather not write about it, but whoever wishes to see it can have it from her children, for they would surely not throw the like of it away.

Only my youngest sister Rebecca, *nebbich*, now remained. But she, too, was married nicely—to the son of my brother-in-law Loeb Hameln in Bonn. An excellent man, this Loeb Bonn presided many years over his and the neighbouring communities, and he likewise possessed a handsome fortune.

Together with his son Samuel, he journeyed to Hamburg where the wedding was celebrated with all merriment, joy and honours. Indeed, one would never have thought that my dear good mother was a widow, for the wedding was carried off as beautifully and splendidly as if my blessed father were still alive. No one of consequence in the community failed to attend, but one and all they came to do her honour.

After the wedding, my brother-in-law Loeb Bonn returned home, and scarcely a half year later he went the way of all the earth. He died in riches and with a good name.

His son Samuel, together with my sister, left for Bonn at once, to enter into his heritage. He prospered there, and befriending everyone, they made him *parnas* in his father's stead.

Some years later, war broke out between the

King of France and Holland and the Kaiser.[13] The French moved against Bonn and captured the city. And Loeb Bonn's house, the heritage from his father, was together with others plundered and burned. He lost all he had, and unable to hold out longer, he came to Hamburg. Much could be written of how he rose again and once more fell, alas, into poverty. Truly he was a pious and God-fearing man. May the Lord help him, and all Israel in their need, and his children too, born and reared in riches and ease, and likewise married—whom fortune, *nebbich*, did not always favour. As the story of King Crœsus teaches us, no man can call himself happy until he dies.

My mother had now married off all of her children in health and honour, to her great content. She was about forty-four years of age when my father died.

Although a number of excellent matches were proposed to her, so that she might have remarried and come into great wealth, the dear and good woman preferred to remain as she was; and with the little that was left to her she quietly made her own way, and lived therefrom decently and well. She dwelt in her own little house, kept her housekeeper by her side, and enjoyed her life in peace. May the good Lord prevail upon every woman, who, God forbid! loses her husband, to do the same.

How contentedly the dear woman lived, the

good she did with her little pittance, her patience in all God gave her to bear—much indeed could be written of it. God grant she continue thus till our Messiah come!

The pleasure we children and her grandchildren took in the dear woman is not to be told. God keep her in health to her hundredth year!

11

We now betrothed our daughter Hannah to Samuel, the son of my brother-in-law Abraham Hameln. Whether it liked us or not, still the match was bestowed of God. For my departed mother-in-law had willed it.

The Frankfort Fair now came round, and my husband, together with Jochanan, Mendel, and Loeb Goslar journeyed to the fair. Straight after its close, they left Frankfort for another fair in Leipzig.

When they reached Fulda, Reb Jochanan fell sick. My husband and Mendel and Loeb Goslar wanted to remain at his side, but the brave good Jochanan would not hear of it. So they continued their journey, while his son Aaron, who had accompanied them, stayed behind. And in four or five days Reb Jochanan died. The sad tidings overtook our travellers before they reached Leipzig, and you can imagine the shock of it.

Shortly thereafter, in Leipzig itself, Reb Mendele, the son of the learned Michael Speyer of Frankfort, laid himself down and within a week he likewise died. You cannot easily picture the fright and dismay that reigned among the Jews.

Not enough they must see a fair young lad torn from the world before his four-and-twentieth year, but his father-in-law, Moses ben Nathan, who was also at the fair, despaired of bringing him to a Jewish grave. For in those days Jews attended Leipzig at their peril, and things went badly with them.

With hard work, with the good offices of influential people and with a great deal of money they at length secured permission to bear away the body. They carried the remains to Dessau, the nearest Jewish community—about thirty miles from Leipzig. It cost over a thousand thalers. But they thanked God they could remove the body from Leipzig.

The news of these misfortunes quickly spread to Hamburg.

Meanwhile, my husband and Loeb Goslar fell sick nigh unto death, and sick as they were had to allow themselves to be transported to Halberstadt. Moses Schnauthan and Issachar Cohen accompanied my husband.

When they reached Halberstadt my husband turned so ill they gave up all hope. Whereupon Issachar Cohen writes me in my husband's name a reassuring letter, bidding me not to take fright, that he lay in no danger, and he pressed my husband till he finally signed it.

But what a signature! No one could have read a letter of it. You may fancy my distress and the anguish of my children.

I received the letter on the first day of the Feast of Weeks. The day before, all the menfolk had returned home from the fair. But not my husband. There wasn't even a letter from him. Instead, the menfolk came to my home immediately on their arrival and begged me not to worry—everything would right itself. But much good that did!

You may picture how we passed our holiday! I could do nothing the day itself, but early next morning I despatched my son Mordecai, Jacob Polack and Chava to Halberstadt, to see if my husband were still among the living. And I fasted and prayed—reproach me not, O Lord!—and otherwise gave myself, as best I could, to penitence, prayer and deeds of mercy.

God, too, took mercy on us and strengthened my husband, that he bettered somewhat and allowed the hiring of a coach. Isaac Kirchhain who was at his side, provided him a bed, so that he could remain lying in the coach on his journey, and still another for his companions.

One at a time they sat in his coach and watched

over him. In this way my husband returned home, broken and suffering.

But we all praised and thanked the dear Lord that «He gave him back unto us and not unto the earth.»[14] The God of goodness prolonged his life another six years, and gave him to see two more of his children married.

12

But I have forgotten to write of the death of my blessed father-in-law; three years, it was, before my husband fell ill in Leipzig.

One day my husband received a letter: «Behold, thy father is sick.»[15] He dropped all his business and hastened to Hanover to visit the sick-bed. He remained a good three weeks in all.

In his eightieth year and shorn, as he was, of his strength, my father-in-law thought that once he had seen my husband again, he would lay himself down and die. For my husband was the youngest child, and he loved him dearly «because he was the son of his old age.»[16]

But when he saw that his son Chayim had been with him three weeks, and it had not yet pleased the Lord to take him, he said to my husband, «My son, I had you come to me in the thought that you would be with me in my last hour. But you are a busy man of affairs and you have already been with me for three weeks. Your duty is done. I am commending myself to God; go you now, in God's name, home to your family!»

Despite my husband's objections and wishes, his father ordered him so emphatically to go home, there was no denying him. The other children, who were by him, were sent home as well.

My husband had not reached Hamburg when the following happened to us:

My daughter Hannah, then eleven years old, slept in a small bed across from mine. I had risen for morning prayers and gone to the synagogue. Meanwhile my little Hannah came running in great fright from her room, quite beside herself with fear. The servants asked her, «What is the matter, Hannah, why do you look so frightened?» Whereat she answered, «I woke up and wanted to see if Mother was in bed, and gracious! there lay an old man with a long white beard. I was terribly scared, and I jumped from bed and ran downstairs. But as I ran out I looked around at the bed, and the old man had raised his head and was looking and looking at me.»

The servants were still in a fluster when I returned from synagogue. I kept on asking what had happened, but no one wanted to tell me.

Two days later my husband returned home, and he was not in the house a week when the news came that his father, the good Reb Joseph, was dead.

My husband's grief and pain cannot be told. Straight after the seven days of mourning he engaged ten Talmud scholars, and fitted up a room in our house where services were held; and he devoted his days and nights to the Torah. He gave up his business travels throughout the whole year of mourning, in order not to miss a single *kaddish* [prayer for the dead].[17]

Twelve weeks following my father-in-law's death, my brother-in-law Isaac Hameln was in Wesel for the wedding of his son Samuel. Thence he went to Hanover to visit his father's grave. The other brothers came too, and wrote my husband to join them. He rose early the next morning and set out for Harburg. He took with him nine companions in order to hold daily prayers, and on the entire journey he did not once fail to say *kaddish*, even though it cost him a good sum of money.

When he came to Hanover he read his father's will. And it was wonderful to behold the wisdom and fear of God written in every line. They also told my husband how my father-in-law died, like a true sage, «as in a kiss»[18]—the death, in truth, of all his godly children.

His children parted their inheritance following every jot and tittle of my father-in-law's last wishes, and no unseemly word rose between them.

My husband remained in Hanover eight days, comforting his mother—as well as he knew how.

He begged her to move with him to Hamburg, but the good woman would not think of it, nor would she leave her pious husband, even in death. Two years later she died, at the age of eighty-two, and was buried next to my father-in-law. The like of this dear couple, blessed of God, will not be found again. May we enjoy the reward of their merits! If only my husband and I could thus have lived out our old age together—but the Most High pleased otherwise.

13

Some time later, my husband found himself in Amsterdam. There he received a proposal for the marriage of our daughter with Moses Krumbach, the son of the rich Abraham Krumbach of Metz.[19] But he had to decide all too quickly. And not till after the betrothal could he write me what was done.

The engagement was concluded in Cleves by Elias Cleve (the father of my son-in-law Kossmann) who had received authority to sign in the name of Abraham Krumbach.

Before my husband wrote me that my daughter Esther was betrothed, I had received letters from several hands, warning me not to conclude the match, for the lad had many, many failings. And then came my husband's letter telling me that the betrothal was signed.

You may well imagine my distress and the sort of joy I took in the match. But I could do nothing until my husband's return.

The next week my husband came home, thinking I should welcome him with open arms and that we would rejoice together over the match. Instead, I greeted him with a heavy heart and could scarcely open my mouth.

My husband remarked at once that something ailed me, but neither of us wished to mar the joy of our reunion. Thus several days passed without our speaking of the marriage.

Meanwhile my husband received a letter from a good friend, who wrote him that he heard the match was on foot and urged him not to enter into it, at least not without first having a look at the young man.

Sorely alarmed, my husband now said to me, «Glückelchen, you too must have known of this, for I have marked your uneasiness.» Whereupon I showed him all the letters I had received before his return. My husband became badly frightened and fell into a gloom. For the young man seemed to have every possible defect. And we had nothing to suggest to each other, for the match was signed.

So I wrote to Frau Jachet, the mother of the lad—I still remember the expressions I used. First, I sent her and her family our friendly greetings. Then I told her we had received sundry letters informing us that her son was afflicted with certain failings. We felt sure it was a lie, and therefore besought her to send the bridegroom, as customary, to a betrothal feast at the home of the bride. And when we had seen, as well we hoped, that liars and slanderers were at work, we would welcome the groom with the greatest joy and pleasure, and neither handsome gifts nor high honours would be spared. But if, God forbid! the truth were other-wise, I begged her not to send us her son, for we would never, so horribly, deceive our child. And should she think to send her son nevertheless, trust-ing that in any case our friendship and kinship would prevail on us to overlook his failings, as sometimes happens, I begged her not to do so. If the reports over her son, God forbid! were true, we must each find reasons for consoling ourselves, and I gave her leave to think all the evil in the world of my daughter . . . and no end of such phrases.

You can imagine how this letter stuck in the crop of the excellent Frau Jachet. She answered in un-varnished wrath and contempt: she had meant, indeed, to have the bridegroom visit the bride, but now that she saw how matters stood, well, if we wished to see her son, we must come ourselves to Metz or send some one in our stead.

Considerable time now passed in exchanging disagreeable letters, to no conclusion. Moreover, the war raging between the King of France and the Reich hindered our visiting one another.

Meanwhile we celebrated our daughter Hannah's marriage with high festival.

I have also forgotten to mention that, a long while before, we happily celebrated the wedding of my son Nathan and Miriam the daughter of the departed Elijah Ballin. My son-in-law Kossmann Cleve and my daughter Zipporah came to the festivities, and we paid all their expenses and made them gifts besides. Jacob Hannover and his wife Süsse were likewise present and many other out-of-town guests, so that it was a truly notable wedding.

This same year saw more than 10,000 Reichsthalers *banko* pass from our hands. But praised be the ever-faithful God, who never failed to restore us our losses, and handsomely! Had He only preserved to me the crown of my head, there would not have been a happier couple in all the world. But because of my great sins and in order that I learn to bow unto His will, the Almighty took my husband to a better and eternal life, and left me in this passing world of woe. We beg our Creator that our end come in accordance with His will and favour, and, please God, He bring us to Paradise.

14

When my husband returned from Hanover after visiting the grave of his father, he found me with child. And throughout my pregnancy he kept hoping I would give birth to a son, that the name of his blessed father be renewed—and praise God, I did.

I will now, my dear children, tell you a true story, which may stand you in good stead.

When young women are with child and see a bit of fruit or the like and feel the slightest yearning for it, let them eat of it at once; otherwise, God forbid, they put their own life in danger or run the risk of deforming their unborn babe—and I know whereof I speak.

I had always laughed and made sport of it when I heard that a woman had come to grief from an unfulfilled desire. I never believed it for a moment; more than that, often enough when I have been with child, and going to the market saw all kinds of fine fruit, and finding it too dear for me, have let it go unbought, I noticed that I never suffered the least harm.

But all days are not alike.[20] This came home to me when I was in the ninth month with my son Joseph. My mother had business on foot with a lawyer living on the Pferdemarkt. So she asked me to accompany her. Although the distance was great and it was close to the time for afternoon prayers —it was, I recall, the beginning of the month of Kislev [November or December]—I had no mind to refuse my mother, and I was still up and about.

So we went downtown together. Opposite the lawyer's house stood a shop where a woman sold medlars. I was always mighty fond of them, so I said to my mother, «Don't forget, on our way home I must buy some medlars.» We then visited the lawyer and did whatever business it was.

But when we finished, it was nearly dark, and hastening on our way we forgot all about the fruit. When I reached home the medlars came to my mind, and I began thinking about them, and it annoyed me I had forgotten to buy them. However, I paid little enough heed to it, no more than when you want to eat something or other that is not in the house.

I went to sleep in excellent spirits, but about midnight my labours began to come upon me. The midwife was summoned, and I gave birth to my son Joseph. The news was quickly carried to my husband, and he had great joy that his father's name lived so soon again.

But the womenfolk who were by me in my labours put their heads together and kept whispering among themselves. I remarked their behaviour, and wanted to know the reason. At last they told me that the babe was covered from head to toes with brown spots. I made them bring a light to my bed, to see for myself. I saw that not only the child was spotted, but he lay in a lifeless heap, moving neither hand nor foot, as though, God forbid, his soul were already taking leave of him. Nor would he suck, nor so much as open his mouth. My husband came and saw it too, and he fell into despair.

This all happened on a Wednesday night, and the circumcision was due a week from Thursday; but we had small hopes of it coming to pass, for the child grew feebler every day. Sabbath came, and, it is true, we celebrated the *Zochor* Feast[21] on Friday night, but we remarked no improvement in the child.

On the close of the Sabbath, while my husband said the *Habdalah* prayers,[22] my mother sat in my room with me. And I said to her, «Please have my Sabbath-woman[23] come to me, I want her to run an errand for me.» My mother asked me what I wanted done, and I told her, «I have been thinking all this while what the reason could be for the brown spots and the feebleness of the babe. And I wondered if my wanting medlars and not getting them were to blame. I came that very night to bed with child. So I'm going to have the woman fetch me a few shillings' worth of medlars, I'll press them to the baby's lips, and, who knows? God may take mercy on us, and with His help the child shall recover.»

My mother waxed very angry with me, and said, «Will you never tire of your nonsense? It is storming tonight as though the heavens would fall, and the woman, be assured, will not set foot outdoors. Moreover, the whole thing is sheer folly.»

But I said to her, «Mother dear, do me the favour and send forth the woman. I will give her whatever she asks, if only I get the medlars—else my heart will know no peace.»

We thereupon called the woman and sent her out for the fruit. She hurried off, but it was a long way and a stormy night not fit for a dog. I thought she never would return, for as always when you wait for something, every second becomes an hour. But at length she returned, along with my medlars.

Because of their bitter taste I knew they were not proper food for a mere babe. Still I ordered the nursemaid to unswathe the child, place it before the fire, and run a bit of the pulp of a medlar around its mouth. Everyone laughed at my folly, but I stood by it, and the nurse must do as I bade. As soon as the fruit touched its lips, the child opened its little mouth so greedily you would have thought it wanted to swallow it all at a gulp, and

it sucked down lustily the pulp of one whole medlar. Yet up till then it wouldn't open its mouth for
a drop of milk, or even a sugar-sop.

Then the nursemaid placed the child by my side,
to see if it would suck. As soon as I put it to my
breast, it began to suck as heartily as a babe of
three months; and from that moment on to the
day of circumcision, all the spots began to leave
its face and body, till only one remained on its
side, about as big as a lentil.

The child appeared for the circumcision healthy,
lusty and well-formed; and, God be praised, it
became a son of Israel at the appointed time. There
followed a circumcision feast which for magnificence had not been seen in Hamburg these many
years. And though my husband had just lost 1000
marks *banko* through the bankruptcy of the Sephardi Isaac Vas, he gave no concern to it, for the
joy he had in his son.

Thus you see, dear children mine, that a woman's
whims are not pure folly and need not always be
despised.

The next time I came with child I suffered terribly. I came down with a fever, God save us! in
my seventh month, an unheard-of thing. If it began in the morning I suffered chills for four whole
hours, then I burned for four hours, and finally,
for four hours again, I sweat, and that was worse

than either the chills or the burning. You may imagine my torments.

I could not eat a bite, though the choicest fare was set before me. Once, of a summer evening, my husband besought me to walk with him by the city wall which lay not far from the house, that I might enjoy a bit of diversion and perhaps recover a taste for food. I told him, «But you know I haven't the strength to walk.» Whereat he said, «The maid and I will drive you there.» I allowed myself to be persuaded, and we drove to the wall, where I sat on the grass.

Meanwhile my husband had ordered Todros, the cook of Manuel Texeira, to prepare a dinner fit for the table of a king. When all was ready we were summoned home, and my husband thought that when I entered the house and found to my surprise the table spread so handsomely and laden with such dainties, I would regain my appetite. But, good God! as soon as I entered the house and set foot in the dining-room, it went so against me, even the mere smell of the food, that I begged them, in mercy's name, either to take the dishes or me from the room.

I continued in this way to suffer torments for two full months. My might failed me, and more than once I thought to myself, «Dear Lord, when my time comes upon me, I shall have neither force nor strength to deliver the child.»

But when my time was on me, the ever-faithful God so graciously lent me His aid, I gave birth almost without pain or effort, as though the child fell of its own will.

It was a lovely, well-built child, but it came down at once with the selfsame fever as mine. Though we summoned doctors and every mortal aid, it proved of no avail. The child suffered fourteen days, and then God took back his share and left us ours, a bit of martyred clay. And me He left, a mother brought to bed—without her babe.

I had two or three further attacks of the fever, but even before I rose from my childbed I was once again healthy and strong.

Thereafter I gave birth to my daughter Hendelchen, and two years later my son Samuel, then my son Moses, my daughter Freudchen, and my daughter Miriam. The two youngest barely knew their father.

What, indeed, shall I write of the gaps betweentimes? Every two years I had a baby, I was tormented with worries as everyone is with a little house full of children, God be with them! and I thought myself more heavily burdened than anyone else in the world and that no one suffered from their children as much as I. Little I knew, poor fool, how fortunate I was when I seated my children «like olive plants round about my table.»[24]

15

My son Mordecai was now grown up, a fine, handsome, well-bred lad. God reward him for the way he honoured his father and mother! But he was well-bred in all things. Once, he accompanied my husband to Leipzig, and my husband fell ill with the colic. No one in Leipzig could tell enough of the wonders he did for his father. He sat by his side all the night, taking neither food, drink nor sleep. Of course he owed as much to his father, but still he was a very young boy. And with God's help they returned home safe and sound.

My husband was never very strong, hence he hastened to marry off his children, in fear of the day that came at last.

So my son Mordecai was betrothed at an early age—his bride was the daughter of the eminent *parnas*, Moses ben Nathan. My husband gave him a dowry of 2000 Reichsthalers, and Moses ben Nathan gave his daughter 3000 Reichsthalers in Danish crown. We shared the wedding costs, amounting to more than 300 Reichsthalers, and we boarded and lodged the young couple for two years at our own expense.

But, alas, not more than six months had passed when my husband's hour had come, and our sins touched their full measure, so that God took from us my good and pious husband, the crown of my head. In the year of Creation 5449 [1689] God's wrath overtook us and my best-beloved was torn from me.

He left me with eight forlorn children, and even the four others already married stood in bitter need of their faithful father.

But what can I say? God had seen my sins, and I needs must lose my dear husband, and my children their most excellent father, and we were abandoned like sheep without a shepherd.

I had always thought I would have the good fortune to be taken first, for during my husband's lifetime I was ever sickly. Whenever I fell ill, the good man used to hope in turn that he would not outlive me. He would say, «How will I be able to take care of the children?»—for he loved them with all his heart.

No doubt, because of his piety God took him first, so that he died in riches and honour and did not live to see evil days. He had attained great wealth, he had married off his children to his satisfaction, and as for himself, he was a true soul and of noble repute. One can say of him, he was a happy man for, as Solon said, he died happy.

Now you know, children of my heart, the story of Reb Chayim Hameln, your dear departed father. How good and beautiful it would have been had God left us together, so that side by side we could have led all our children beneath the wedding canopy! But my sins found me out, and I was not worthy of it.

He left me in desolation, and my woes came «new every morning.»[25] I shall tell thereof in my fifth book, alas, a book of bitter lament, like the lamentation for Zion.

The money and goods my husband bequeathed me, though plentiful enough, are as naught against this uncountable loss.

Now I will close my fourth book—may God bring us joy again, as He has brought me sorrow, and Thou one and only God, have mercy on my orphaned children!

THE END OF MY FOURTH BOOK

BOOK FIVE

1

I BEGIN this fifth book, dear children, with a heavy heart, for I mean to tell, from beginning to end, of the sickness and death of your beloved father.

The evening of the 19th of Tebet, 5449 [January 11, 1689], your father went into town to arrange certain business with a merchant. When he was close to the merchant's house, he stumbled and fell over a sharp stone, and hurt himself so badly we were all alarmed.

He came home in great agony. I chanced to be visiting my mother, and I was called back at once. I found my husband groaning by the fire, and badly frightened, I asked him what had happened. He told me he had fallen, and feared there was much for me to do. He was unable to stir, and I had to empty his pockets myself. For when he set forth he had laden them with jewellery.

We did not at once, God help us! know the real nature of his injury. He had long suffered from a rupture, and in stumbling he had fallen on the ruptured spot and badly twisted his bowels.

A bed stood always ready in the lower room, but he did not wish to use it, and we had to bring him upstairs to the bed-chamber. It was a bitter cold night, as though the skies would freeze together, and we remained by his side through the cold hours, doing our best for him. But we could stand it no longer, it did him no good either to lie there in the cold, and at last he saw the harm of it, and we brought him downstairs once more.

We worried along in this way until past midnight, and still he grew no better. I saw my sorrowful fate staring me in the face, and I begged him, in Heaven's name, to let us call a doctor and attendants. Whereat he said, «I would rather die than let the world know of it.» I stood before him and wept and screamed, «What talk is this?» I said, «Why shouldn't people know? It has come through no shame or sin.»

But my talk proved all of no avail. He clung to the foolish fancy that it might do his children harm; people would say that the weakness was in the blood. For he never had thought of else than his children. And so we had to contend with him the livelong night, and applying every manner of poultice.

When day broke, I said to him, «Praise God the night is over, now I will send for a doctor

and a rupture-cutter.» But he would not listen
to it, and bade me send for the Sephardi Abraham
Lopez, a physician and chirurgeon-barber. I had
him fetched at once.

When he came and saw the injury, he said,
«Have no fear. I will lay on something that will
heal him forthwith. I have dealt with hundreds
like him, and it has never failed me.»

This was early Wednesday morning. Dr. Lopez
applied his remedy, thinking it would shortly heal
him. But, God have mercy! when noontime came,
he said, «My cure, I see, is not enough—I will go
and bring a rupture-cutter whom I know to have
a clever hand.» The rupture-cutter came and
worked the entire day in the hope of easing the
injury. But the longer he laboured, the worse it
became.

Thursday I brought in another rupture-cutter
and two more physicians, one of them Dr. Fon-
seca. When I talked with him and related all the
circumstances, he told me, «There is little I can
say—or do. Alas, the bowels are so badly twisted
he will not be able to evacuate.» And what should
have gone off naturally broke, God help us! through
the open wound. Every aid failed him, and still
he refused to have strangers about him and begged
us all to keep it a secret. As for me, I knew and
saw my fate before my eyes.

So Thursday passed, day and night, in bitter

distress. Friday Dr. Lopez brought us a Berlin doctor, for many years physician to the Elector. He
too gave him something to take and laid on a
bandage, alas, to no purpose.

It was Saturday morning when my brother-in-
law Joseph first learned that something was wrong
with my blessed husband. He came running to
our house and begged to be let into the sick-room.
When my husband heard him, he said, let him
enter.

As soon as Joseph saw him, *nebbich*, he knew
what it meant. He struck his head against the
wall and tore his hair and with bitter tears he
cried aloud, «Woe unto me that I must lose a
brother-in-law like him!» And he cast himself on
my husband's bed, and with streaming eyes begged
his forgiveness for aught he had done.

My husband answered him from the bottom of
his heart. «My beloved brother-in-law,» he said,
«I forgive you and all living men, and give me, I
pray, your forgiveness too.» Whereat my brother-
in-law sought to calm him and bade him be patient,
God would yet come to his aid. And my husband
replied, he was content to be in God's hands.

As for myself, he did not tell me a half of his
illness, but he kept ever at his side my son Loeb,
then a lad of sixteen. When I was out of the room,
he called the lad to him and told him how matters
stood, and the boy wept sorely. But as soon as my

husband marked I had returned, he quickly said to the boy, «Silence, for the mercy of God! Your mother comes—let her not see your tears!» Even at death's door he thought of nothing but to spare me pain.

Saturday morning, after meal-time, my mother came and flung herself upon him, and kissing him between her tears, she said, «My son, must you now abandon us? Is there naught I may do for you?» Whereat he answered, «You know I have loved you like a mother—I have naught to ask or to say—only comfort my poor Glückelchen.» That was the last word he spoke to her.

But who is now my comforter? To whom shall I pour out my soul? Whither shall I turn? All his life my beloved companion hearkened to my troubles, and they were many, and comforted me so that somehow they would quickly vanish. But now, alas, I am left to flounder in my woe.

Later, more doctors and rupture-cutters came, but they could do nothing. By the close of the Sabbath, no one remained but Dr. Lopez and myself.

Towards midnight Dr. Lopez sent for a chirurgeon, in the hope that the wound was fit; but he came and saw at a glance that nothing could be done, and he departed.

Whereat I said to my husband, «Dearest heart, shall I embrace you—I am unclean?» For I was then at a time I dared not touch him. And he said, «God forbid, my child—it will not be long before you take your cleansing.» But, alas, it was then too late.[1]

Upon the advice of Dr. Lopez I now summoned Feibisch Levi who knew how to be with a man in his dying hour. He arrived towards two in the morning, when I also called in our teacher, a most trustworthy man.

Feibisch Levi went at once to my husband. «Reb Chayim,» he said, «have you any last wishes to give us?» Whereat my husband answered, «None. My wife knows everything. She shall do as she has always done.» And then he asked Reb Feibisch to bring him the works of the learned Rabbi Isaiah Hurwitz.[2]

After he had read in them for about half an hour, he turned to Reb Feibisch and our teacher. «Don't you see,» he said, «how near I am? Let my wife and children leave. It is high time.» Whereupon Reb Feibisch thrust us by main force from the room.

Reb Feibisch now sought to engage him in further talk. He gave no answer, but began speaking to himself. They could only see his lips moving. So it was for nearly another half-hour, and then Reb Feibisch said to Dr. Lopez, «Abraham my friend, lay your ear to his mouth, perchance you can hear what he is saying.» Dr. Lopez did so, and after a space he heard him say, «Hear, O Israel, the Lord our God, the Lord is One!» With that, his breath ceased and he had breathed away his pure soul.

Thus he died in purity and holiness, and they saw from his end the man that he was.

2

What shall I write, dear children, of all our bitter grief? I had always stood so high in his eyes, and now I was abandoned with eight of my twelve forlorn children—and one of them, my daughter Esther, betrothed! May God have mercy on us and be the Father of my children, for He is the Father of the fatherless! I truly believe I shall never cease from mourning my dear friend.

Sunday, the 24th of Tebet, 5449 [January 16, 1689], he was buried with all honour. The entire community was struck with horror and grief at the sudden blow of it.

With my children gathered around me, I sat upon the ground for the seven days of mourning, and a sad sight it must have been to see me sitting thus with my twelve fatherless children by my side.

We immediately secured our ten men for the daily prayers in the house of mourning, and we engaged scholars to «learn» Torah day and night through the whole year—be it not to my reproach! And the children diligently said *kaddish* for their departed father. And there was not a man or woman who did not come, daily, to comfort the bereaved among us.

And, alas, there was no dearth of tears. We passed the seven days of mourning as you may only too well imagine. «I fed on the bread of tears and drank tears in great measure» . . . «What thing shall I liken to thee, O daughter of Jerusalem?»[3]

I was «cast down from heaven unto the earth.»[4] Thirty years I had enjoyed my beloved husband and he had bestowed on me all that a true wife could want. And he had, as I might say, thought of me after his death, so I could lift my head in honour. But what does this all avail me? The decrees of Heaven cannot be changed.

Still, dear children, our good friend died the death of the righteous. He lay but four days on his bed and kept his mind undimmed until he breathed his soul away. «Let my last end be like his,»[5] and may his merits stand us in our need! He had the good fortune to leave this sinful world in honours and riches, and lived to see no unhappiness in his children. For «the righteous is taken away from the evil to come.»[6]

But when his soul took wing, there flew with it all my glory, wealth and honour. And I remained behind with my single and married children, steeped in care and woe which every day grew greater. «My friends and my kinsmen stand aloof from my sore.»[7] Aye, my sins had brought me to this pass; and I shall never forget him as long as I live, for he lies buried in my heart.

My dear mother and her children sought to comfort me, but it was as oil poured upon fire, and my grief grew only the worse for it.

Visits of consolation kept on for two or three weeks; and then everyone forgot all about me, and the very people we had helped most began to repay us with evil, as is the way of the world. At least I fancied so—for a widow, God forgive me! who has of a sudden lost her all is quick to see and take offence, and often unjustly.

The days, my beloved children, that the dear friend of my heart lay dead before me were not as bad as those that followed. Then it was my grief deepened hourly. But in His mercy the great and good God at length brought me patience, so that I have taken care of my fatherless children as far as a weak woman can, bowed with affliction and woe.

3

After the thirty days of mourning, neither brother nor sister nor one of my kin came to see me and ask, what will you do? or how will you manage? When we had chanced to meet during the thirty days, their advice was fruitless and of little use to me or my desolate children.

My husband had not willed to appoint a guardian, as (I told you) he said to Reb Feibisch. So, after the thirty days, I went over my books and discovered we owed 20,000 Reichsthalers of debts. It was not news to me and gave me no worry, for I knew I could pay them and still have enough to provide for myself and my children.

Yet it was no light thing for a widow to be weighed with such debts, and not even a hundred thalers cash in the house. My sons Nathan and Mordecai came, like true children, to my aid, but they were still young. So I put everything together, balanced my accounts, and decided to call an auction, which presently took place.

My dear children, you have seen how your father took leave of this sinful world, your shepherd and your friend. Hereafter, trust only to yourselves, for now there is no man and no friend on whom you may depend, and even had you many friends, if you needed their aid you could not rely on them. For when a man has no need thereof, everyone wishes to befriend him, but when he stands in want of friends they are not, as the story goes, to be found.

Once upon a time, a king sent his son to a far country to learn wisdom. After thirteen years the king wrote him it was time to come home, and welcomed him with a royal feast. And he asked the prince, «Had you many friends, my son, in the city where you learned wisdom?» Whereat the son said, «The whole city were my friends.» «And how,» the king asked, «did they become your friends?» «Every day,» answered the son, «I had them dine with me and gave them of the finest wine.»

The king sighed and shook his head. «I thought,» he said, «you had learned wisdom. But you have not even learned that pot-brothers are not friends. Anyone will be your devoted friend as long as you give him good food and fine drinks. But when you ply him no longer or when he finds better fare elsewhere, both he and his friendship vanish.»

Whereupon the prince asked, «My lord and father, who then is the dependable friend and where may he be found?» The king replied, «Call no man a true friend until you have tried him.» «And how may I try him?» asked the son.

For answer, the king bade his son kill a young calf, place the body in a sack, and carry it secretly by night to whomever he thought a friend, and tell the friend that the sack contained the body of the lord high chamberlain whom he had killed in a brawl, and beg the friend help him dispose of the body and conceal the murder.

The prince did so, and of all his intimates and

liegemen only his valet offered him help in his need. And he would go no further than to keep watch on a byway while the prince buried the sack by himself.

And the prince returned to his father and said, «I have learned more wisdom in one night than in thirteen years abroad, and among all my liegemen I have found only one friend, my valet, and he is but half a one. Tell me, now, what shall I do to reward him?»

«The best way to reward him,» said the king, «is to give all your other servants a thrashing.» «But why,» asked the son, «punish my servants for doing no wrong?»

«If a wise man,» answered the king, «were surrounded by a thousand fools, and there was no other way of enabling him to escape, I should advise one to kill the thousand fools. So I advise you to thrash your witless servants, that your valet who is now a half friend may become your full friend.»

We, my children, have no friend on whom we may depend, save God, who will ever stand by you and aid you. You have lost your true and good father, but your Heavenly Father abideth forever, and He will not desert you as long as you serve Him in faithfulness. And if, God forbid, you suffer punishment, you will have naught to blame but yourself and your own deeds.

4

I told you how I cast up my accounts. Thereafter I went to my brother-in-law Joseph and
begged him go over my stock and see if perchance
I had set too high or low a price on the various
items. He looked at everything and said, «You
have valued it all too cheaply. Were I to sell my
goods at such prices I should go bankrupt.» But
I told him, «Methinks it is wiser to set a low value
on my goods and have them go at a higher price
than the other way around. As it is, I have reckoned
that even sold as cheaply as I have marked them,
they will yield me an excellent capital for my
fatherless children.»

Then I held my auction, and it passed off very
happily. Everything brought a good price, and
though I allowed six months for payment, still it
all went nicely, and praise God, I suffered no losses.

As soon as money began to come in, I set to
paying my debts, and within a year I was clear
of them. The balance, as it came to my hands, I
loaned out at interest.

My daughter Esther, I have told you, was even
then long betrothed, and we found means neither
of breaking nor of consummating the match. Hard
upon my thirty days of mourning, I wrote the
groom's mother in Metz, telling her of my unhappy
widowhood and begging her despatch us her son,

that we might see him and put an end to our differences. But she answered me, I had written such evil of her son and she had heard such things of my daughter, she had no wish to send me the groom. If I believed the slanders heaped upon her son, I only need send to Metz one of my friends to see for himself. Moreover, she wrote me, the war between the King of France and the Reich made it far too dangerous for her son to travel. So for more than a year the match advanced no further than the passage of unpleasant letters.

My son Loeb had now grown into a big handsome youth, and he received numerous proposals. My brother-in-law Joseph talked to me himself in behalf of his daughter, and bade us make our own terms. But it misliked my son, who preferred a Berlin match, to his and all our undoing. Yet I blame no one. The Most High had decreed our fate, and taken away my husband e'er he could live to see the misfortunes of his children.

Youth-like, my son Loeb had allowed himself to be misled by loose companions into a great deal of nonsense and folly. So I thought to myself: If he marries in Hamburg the seduction will only be greater. I am a widow and the people here are busy with big affairs and have no time to watch over him.

Meanwhile, my brother-in-law Elias Ries had proposed the daughter of his brother Hirschel Ries in Berlin. The match, alas, pleased me at once. I said to myself, the man has few children and he conducts most of his business at home, moreover, he is a stern man and would take good care of my son.

So I betrothed my son to his daughter, and thought I had done very well.

When the wedding drew near. I set forth, together with the bridegroom, Issachar Cohen, my brother-in-law Elias Ries, and my son Samuel, for Berlin, where we were the guests of Benjamin Mirels.

I cannot describe the honours heaped on me by Hirschel Ries, his uncle Benjamin Mirels, and everyone in Berlin, above all the honours showed me by the rich Judah Berlin and his wife. Though Judah Berlin had fallen out with the Vienna Jews,[8] he sent me on Sabbath the finest sweetmeats a man could buy, and gave a magnificent dinner for me. In brief, I received more honours than I deserved.

We celebrated the wedding with great joy and in all pomp. And some days later we all returned merrily to Hamburg.

Before I left Berlin I spoke with Hirschel Ries and begged him keep a close eye on my son, for he was still a lad who knew nothing as yet of business. I had, I told him, consented to the marriage because I hoped my son would find in him another father. Whereat Hirschel Ries assured me

I need nowise worry for my son, I need only wish to have as few fears for my other children. But, O my God and Lord, what was I to see on the turning of the page!

Hirschel Ries had pledged himself, in the betrothal-contract, to board and house my son for three years, and to lay by 400 Reichsthalers yearly for him. But he kept his word no better in this promise than the other.

Meanwhile, the letters with regard to my daughter Esther's match continued to pass to no purpose. Since the groom and his father would not or could not come to Hamburg, and since I and my daughter refused to go to Metz, we finally agreed that *parnas* Abraham Krumbach, the wealthy father of the groom, should accompany his son to Amsterdam. And I in turn undertook to bring the bride, and after they had looked upon and found each other to their liking, the wedding should be held forthwith.

So I set forth with my daughter Esther and my son Nathan, and reached Amsterdam at the proper time. We went in good company and enjoyed a pleasant and lovely journey.

We put up in Amsterdam with my son-in-law Kossmann Cleve, and the bridegroom, who had arrived a little before us, stayed with Moses Emmerich.

Towards evening, following the afternoon

prayers, the bridegroom came to our house. I was mighty happy and talked with him for a long space, and in every respect he pleased me. I found not one of the defects people had laid to his account. We remained together two or three hours, and I thanked God from my heart and was mighty content.

While we were in Amsterdam, my son and I did business every day in precious stones.

After we were there a week, I received a letter from Frau Miriam, the wife of the departed Elias Cleve, bidding us do her the honour of coming to Cleves with the bridal couple. Since it was she who had undertaken the match and had reaped little but annoyances from it, the least we could do was to meet her wishes and pay her a visit.

Although it was hard to break off our business dealings, still I could not refuse her invitation, and we all journeyed to Cleves. When we met we both broke down in tears, for it was the first time we had seen each other since we had been reduced to widowhood. But after the first shock was over, cheer and good spirits prevailed, and we took great pleasure in one another. My daughter Zipporah was likewise with us.

Frau Miriam had wished the wedding to be celebrated in Amersfoort, but the place hardly suited me, for we were compelled in any case to return to Amsterdam.

We passed five happy days in Cleves, and then we all set out, together with the bridal pair, for Amsterdam. Once there, the wedding preparations were set on foot, and while we had planned on only thirty or forty guests, over four hundred attended. In brief, so magnificent a wedding had not been seen in Amsterdam these hundred years. It cost us, too, more than 400 Reichsthalers.

I remained in Amsterdam some weeks after the celebration, attending to business. Then we made ready for the journey home. I had begged my new son-in-law Moses to return with us and offered them my roof, but he refused. So we arrived content in Hamburg and found our children and friends in the best of health.

5

I had received a letter from my son Loeb in every post, and heard that he was doing nicely in business; everyone, in fact, was exclaiming at his talents as a business man. He attended the Leipzig Fair where he made excellent purchases, and had a large store in Berlin. My other children likewise did business with him.

I wrote frequently to his father-in-law Hirschel Ries as to whether he was content with my son, for the lad was still young and strange to business, having passed his life in the *cheder* [Hebrew primary school] and *beth ha-midrash* [study-room of synagogue]. And just as frequently Hirschel Ries answered me, I need give myself no concern. I had to be satisfied, and I believed that all was going well with my son.

My daughter Hendele was now a grown-up girl, good and beautiful as could be. Whereupon the marriage broker Reb Josel proposed us another unhappy Berlin match. There dwelt in Berlin the widow of Baruch Veit, who died a rich and honoured man and left two sons and two daughters.

The broker proposed me the eldest son for my Hendele. He assured me the young man was an excellent lad, he was studious, he had 5000 Reichsthalers cash, besides half a house worth another 1500 Reichsthalers, and silver Torah decorations and other things. His mother intended to keep him at her side and give him two years' board at her table, for she was still deeply engaged in business.

I told the broker I did not refuse the proposal, but wished to consider it and then give him my answer. I now consulted my brother-in-law Joseph and other good friends. They advised me to accept, but they one and all said, you have your son in Berlin who can write you everything.

So I wrote my son Loeb, bidding him send me a full report. He replied advising the marriage, for the young man had the 5000 Reichsthalers and everything else the broker had claimed. Whereat I sent my son full powers and he signed the betrothals—to my great sorrow. The wedding was fixed for a year and six months later.

I thought all was well, and I said to myself, since I have one child doing nicely in Berlin I shall marry off thither a second, that one may take joy in the other. But, alas, it turned out far otherwise.

For my son Loeb, I told you, was still a lad and knew nothing of business. And his father-in-law, far from keeping a steady eye on him, let him run like a loose sheep.

As I mentioned, my son had undertaken a large business in Berlin, with a big store full of all manner of goods. His father-in-law, likewise, had married his son Model to the daughter of my brother-in-law Joseph. This Model was also a raw lad and poorly bred. But his father placed his entire dowry of 4000 Reichsthalers in my son's business.

My son kept this Model sitting in the store, that is to say, watching out for things. But what a watchman! The help, men and women, stole right and left. Other worthless folk, such as are to be found in Berlin and thereabouts, made up to him, and while they went through the motions of bargaining stole from under his eyes.

In addition, my son Loeb loaned some thousands to Polish Jews, and the money, alas, was never seen again.

My children and I knew nothing of it all, we

thought he was doing a good as well as a big business, and so we made him large advances. At that time I had a manufactory for Hamburger stockings, many thousands' worth of which I turned out for my own account. And my unlucky son writes me to send him a thousand thalers and more of stockings, and I did so.

Then I meet at the Brunswick Fair certain Amsterdam merchants who hold my son's notes for about 800 Reichsthalers. My son Loeb writes me I can safely take up the notes—he will forward me the money to Hamburg. As I always stood by my children, I said to myself, I shall not put him to shame by protesting the notes, and I proudly paid them.

When I returned from the Brunswick Fair I expected to find bills of exchange from my son Loeb. But nothing awaited me, and when I wrote to him, he sent me all kinds of answers none of which pleased me. What was I to do? I needs must content myself.

Two weeks later, a good friend came to me and said, «I cannot keep it from you, I must tell you that your son Loeb's business mislikes me, for he is heavily plunged in debt. He owes his brother-in-law Model 4000 Reichsthalers, and Model sits in his store, that is to say, he watches after things. But he is a child and cannot attend to his business. He is out gulping food and drink at all hours and everyone is lord and master of the store. Your son Loeb is too nice and good, and easily led by the nose. Added to that, the Berliners are bleeding him with their interest. Moreover, he has two wolves at his flanks, one is that Wolf Mirels—son of the Hamburg rabbi Solomon Mirels—and the other is Wolf the brother-in-law of the learned Benjamin Mirels. Every day this second Wolf goes to the store and makes off with what he pleases. Finally, your son does business with Polish Jews, so much so, I know, that he has already rid himself of more than 4000 thalers.»

Such and more of the like my good friend told me, and my soul nearly died within me, and I fainted on the spot.

When my friend saw my shock, he tried to console me and said he believed that with some one to stand by him my son could still be saved.

I told all I had heard to my sons Nathan and Mordecai. They shrank with fright and said he owed them several thousands. God knows what it meant for me—my son Loeb owed me alone more than 3000 Reichsthalers—but I had little minded it were not his brothers so deeply immersed. But what could we do in our distress? We dare speak of it to no one.

We agreed that I should accompany my son Mordecai to the Leipzig Fair and see how matters stood. When we reached Leipzig we found my son

Loeb already on hand, as was his wont, and laden with goods.

I now began to talk with him. «They are saying,» I said, «thus and so of you. Bethink yourself of God and of your good and honest father, that you bring us not to shame.» He answered, «You need not worry over me. But recently—it was not a month ago—my father-in-law had visiting him his brother-in-law Wolf of Prague, and we reckoned up my accounts and he found me, praise God, in excellent shape.» Whereat I said to him, «Show me your balance sheet.» He replied, «I haven't it with me; but do me the favour to come to Berlin and I will show you everything, to your content.» «In any case,» I concluded, «buy not a jot more of goods.»

But my back was no sooner turned than Reb Isaac and Reb Simon, son of Rabbi Mann of Hamburg, sold him on credit more than 1400 thalers of goods. When I learned of it, I went to them and begged them in Heaven's name withdraw the sale, for my son needs must give over the merchandise trade, else it be his ruin. But it was all to no purpose, and they forced my son to take the wares.

After the fair, I accompanied my son Mordecai, Hirschel Ries and the other Berliners to Berlin.

Once I was in his house, my son Loeb said to me, «I fancy my one mistake is to have tied up too much money in goods.» Whereupon I told him, «You owe me more than 3000 Reichsthalers —for my part I am satisfied to take it in goods at the price they cost you.» «Mother dear,» he said, «if you are willing to do that, it will ease me of my difficulties, and no one need lose a penny through me.»

The next day I went with my son to his store, and truly, he was badly overladen with goods. He gave me 3000 Reichsthalers of merchandise at the price it cost him. And you can imagine the face I made. But regardless of everything, I only sought to help my children.

We had the goods packed in bales to send on to Hamburg. Then I noticed the two bales of goods my son had bought in Leipzig from Reb Isaac and Reb Simon the Hamburg merchants, and I said to my son, «Send back those two bundles of goods, and I shall see to it they are accepted, even if I pay for them from my own pocket. And now,» I continued, «that you have repaid your debt to me, what of my sons Nathan and Mordecai?» He had on hand bills of exchange and Polish paper amounting to over 12,000 Reichsthalers, and he gave them to my son Mordecai by way of payment.

After sitting the whole day in his store, we went home together; and you would be right in thinking I did not enjoy my supper.

Very early next morning my son Loeb comes to me in my room and says, his father-in-law refuses to allow the goods to leave Berlin inasmuch as my son owes Model 4000 Reichsthalers, but once I pay him this money I might send the goods where I please. My son told me this with streaming eyes.

Of a sudden, mortal agony and fear lay hold on me, so that my limbs failed me, and as long as I remained in that cursed city I could not rise from my bed.

I bade Hirschel Ries come to me, and I told him what he was doing, and asked him if he meant to slay my son and me at a stroke.

But why try to write of it all? Ten sheets wouldn't begin to hold it. I was forced to give Hirschel Ries a note for 2500 Reichsthalers, payable within two weeks at Hamburg.

At this Hirschel Ries proceeded to say, «I hope no one is caught with a loss, for your son still holds large stocks of goods. Besides the store here, he has some 2000 Reichsthalers' worth of goods standing in Frankfort-on-the-Oder, in addition to the bills and paper in the hands of your son Mordecai.»

What remained to be done? We must take it all in good grace. I signed the notes and thereupon shipped my goods to Hamburg. Then I accompanied Hirschel Ries to the store and showed him the two bundles from Reb Isaac and Reb Simon, and bade him return them at once, that my son be relieved of the obligation.

The bills and paper in my son Mordecai's posses-

sion proved of little use; we turned them over to
Hirschel Ries, who gave his hand he would remit
to Hamburg whatever came of them.

My son Loeb likewise owed Loeb Beschere and
Loeb Goslar around 2000 Reichsthalers, and he gave
me from the bills of exchange enough to repay
them. I could have withheld them for my own
account, but I considered that if I did the like,
my son were surely bankrupt. And so I placed
them in the proper hands.

We now journeyed home, downcast and in bitter
spirits. I had little life in me. My dear and good
son Mordecai sought to comfort me, but, God wot,
he was more distressed than I, and, alas, he plainly
showed it.

The Frankfort-on-the-Oder Fair drew near, and
therein we placed all our hopes for retrieving ourselves. But instead, Hirschel Ries descended on my
son's store and seized everything he had—not alone
his goods but all his bills of exchange and the two
bundles promised for Hamburg. Not a penny remained for us or for my son Loeb.

Alas, what is more, my son was owing a merchant 1000 Reichsthalers, for which he proposed
to give him bills on Hamburg. But the merchant
learned how matters stood, and refusing any clemency, wanted to thrust him behind the bars.

What should my son do? His father-in-law
would have let him rot in prison e'er he would

have helped him with a hundred thalers, to say nothing of a thousand. So my son said to the merchant, «You can see for yourself there is nothing here for you. Let me go with you to Hamburg where my mother and my brothers will not forsake me. After all, you can, if needs be, lock me up in Hamburg.»

Whereupon my son wrote me, «I shall arrive Friday—I cannot write the reasons—I will tell you all by word of mouth.»

I received the letter a day before his arrival. It is not hard to picture my distress. I knew that it boded nothing good, that his father-in-law had taken everything, that he owed large debts in Hamburg, and that he had nothing wherewith to pay them.

But I had little time to dwell on my forebodings. Early Friday morning came a message that my son Loeb was at the merchant's house and that either I or my children should come to him. I was frightened beyond all measure and could not stir a step. My son Mordecai set off instead, and brought me back the woeful tidings.

I now consulted my brothers-in-law Joseph and Elias as to what could be done. If the matter continued much longer and the other creditors got wind of it, my son was lost.

We finally concluded to take a thousand thalers from the estate, to free him from the hands of the merchant. He was to remain till dark at the merchant's house and then till Sunday at our own. The first thing Sunday morning I was to send him, together with my brother-in-law Samuel Bonn, to Hameln where he might remain at the home of my son-in-law Samuel Hameln until we saw what was intended against him.

And so it was done, and again it cost me a large sum of money.

My son Loeb set forth for Hameln, and on the road he stopped, of necessity, at Hanover. Though my nephew, the rich Jacob Hannover son of Leffmann Behrens, proffered him much sympathy, nothing in the way of help came of it. They wrote me consoling letters, and I answered beseemingly and thanked them for their consolation, but told them that something more was needed, and suggested they intercede in my son's behalf, that he come clear of his difficulties. I received for answer a letter from Jacob Hannover; he offered to aid with 500 Reichsthalers provided my sons Nathan and Mordecai would promise him in writing to go surety for the money.

Again you may learn to hold no man a friend till you have tried him. I had believed that Jacob Hannover, who held himself a close friend of my child, would have done more, for the honour of my husband, aye, given thousands for the honour of his uncle; but he did as I have said.

Six months passed and my son Loeb remained in Hameln. A little thereafter, the Elector of Brandenburg journeyed to Hanover. I heard of it at once and wrote my brother-in-law Leffmann Behrens to undertake to procure a letter of safe-conduct for my son. With this he might return to Berlin and learn something of his affairs and pacify his creditors.

For my son was well liked among both Jews and Gentiles, and they knew that frivolous and wicked men—may their names be blotted out!—had despoiled him because of his big and trusting heart.

There remained sundry small claims on him from which he could have disentangled himself, and he thought God would take pity on him and bring him to his feet again. But Heaven, it seemed, was still wroth with us.

My son Loeb now set forth for Berlin, where he ran quacking about and trying to do a little business. But as fast as he stopped up one hole he opened another, thinking all the while, as such folk do, that he was mending matters.

6

A Berlin match, as I have told you, was concluded for my dear good daughter at a time we believed my son to be prospering. But when it all turned out so unhappily, the thought of Berlin went against me. Moreover, my son Loeb told me that the bridegroom fell a good deal short of what he had written. Although my son had wished to warn me of it at the outset, he was already in straits and the parents of the young man had helped him with money (to his downfall!), and they had forced him to write me as he did.

I now spoke with my friends and other folk, for the unfortunate wedding was rapidly drawing near. They sent me word from Berlin that the bridegroom had nothing but 3500 thalers and his half of a house, whereat I wanted to break the match, since it did not fulfil the promises made in the betrothal-contract.

Letters and demands and counter-demands consumed more than a year, until at length I was, God be my judge, dragged into it by the hair of my head and forced to take my daughter to Berlin and marry her forthwith.

Her dowry was loaned out at interest in Hamburg, and the dowry of the groom was likewise placed at interest in the hands of trustworthy Berliners. Although I set forth with little enough joy, not merely because of my son Loeb but out of plain distaste for the marriage, still I mastered myself and allowed naught to escape me that would mar the happiness of my child.

I put up with my son Loeb, and his lot was pitiable. He had done his best and run his legs off— to what purpose I have said; and for all that my heart sank within me, I determined to give no sign of my distress.

Thus, if you will, the wedding passed off in all merriment, joy and honour.

The rich Judah Berlin, together with his wife and all the friends of his house, honoured us with his presence at the ceremony, to the great astonishment of everyone, for he had hitherto never deigned attend a wedding among the Vienna Jews. He likewise gave her a costly wedding-present, and after the marriage invited the bridal pair to a stately dinner.

When all was over we made ready to return home, but with a heavy heart, for the fate of my son stood before my eyes. Yet I clung to the hope that God might come to his aid and retrieve him.

So we set forth for Hamburg, and I left behind me my good and beloved daughter. And I never saw her again. The pain of our parting cannot be told; it was as though we had known we should meet no more in this world below. And so we bade farewell forever.

After my arrival home, I received letters from my daughter in every post, and seemingly happy ones. Although she too grieved and worried for my son Loeb, the good and pious child spoke no word of it and sought to spare me further sorrow. It was as though she locked her grief within her own pure heart.

My son Loeb swiftly reached the point where he must leave Berlin. He found refuge in Altona under the protection of the President.[9] The heartaches I suffered at his lot and the troubles his creditors bestowed upon me, let them serve as penance for my sins! Every day saw money torn from me.

Then my son fell grievously ill, and I had to send two doctors daily to Altona, besides attendants and other needs. Again this cost me much money. But in the end he recovered.

Next, my good daughter Hendele fell sick in Berlin, and needs must pay for it with her young blood, to my utter desolation and the anguish of all who knew her. The punishment, O my God! was nigh more than I could bear. So dear and true a child, slender as a pine-tree, and all of innocent love and piety, like unto the holy mothers of our tribe! I cannot find the words to tell of the grief of all Berlin, and not the least her mother-in-law who loved her as her own. Yet what did it all avail my mother's heart? It was only seventeen weeks after her wedding. But I shall not open my wounds anew.

After the seven days of mourning my son Loeb had word brought to me, bidding me come to Altona. I went, and we both wept, and he comforted me as best he could.

Then he said to me, «Mother dear, how will my sorry plight end? I am a young man, yet I spend my days in idleness. My dear sister died childless, and her husband must, therefore, return the dowry, which will go to my brothers. Should they only this once take pity on me and help me with their dowry money so I may satisfy my creditors and return to Hamburg, I believe I can with God's help get to my feet again.»

My full heart sank at his words, and I could not answer him for bitter tears. Presently I said to him: «How can you think of such a wrong? Well you know that your brothers have already come to grief through you, in truth they can no longer support their losses; and now when a bit of tear-stained money, alas, returns to them, you want to snatch it from their bitterly aching hearts.»

And then, for an hour together, the both of us pitifully screamed and quarrelled—until at length our words gave out.

Silently I gathered my Hamburger shawl about me, and with tears and bitter heart betook myself home. I said nothing of it to my children, but my son Loeb did not fail to send for them and kept at them with his prayers until, generous souls that they were, they promised to do his will.

So, in a short while, he came to an agreement with his creditors and returned to me in Hamburg. Quickly as his father-in-law heard of it, he de-spatched his daughter, Loeb's wife, together with her child, likewise to my house, and gave his daughter two Reichsthalers a week for pin-money. There was naught for me to do save to take it all with the best mien I could.

At that time I was busied in the merchandise trade, selling every month to the amount of five or six hundred Reichsthalers. Further, I went twice a year to the Brunswick Fair and each time made my several thousands profit, so in all, had I been left in peace, I would have soon repaired the loss I suffered through my son.

My business prospered, I procured me wares from Holland, I bought nicely in Hamburg as well, and disposed of the goods in a store of my own. I never spared myself, summer and winter I was out on my travels, and I ran about the city the livelong day.

What is more, I maintained a lively trade in seed pearls. I bought them from all the Jews, selected and assorted them, and then resold them in towns where I knew they were in good demand.

My credit grew by leaps and bounds. If I had wanted 20,000 Reichsthalers *banko* during a session of the Bourse, it would have been mine.

«Yet all this availeth me nothing.»[10] I saw my son Loeb, a virtuous young man, pious and skilled in Talmud, going to pieces before my eyes.

One day I said to him, «Alas, I see nothing ahead of you. As for me, I have a big business, more indeed than I can manage. Come then, work for me in my business and I will give you two per cent of all the sales.»

My son Loeb accepted the proposal with great joy. Moreover, he set to work diligently, and he could soon have been on his feet had not his natural bent led him to his ruin. He became, through my customers, well known among the merchants, who placed great confidence in him. Nearly all my business lay in his hands.

7

My son Joseph was then a youngster of fourteen, a fine lad and exceedingly apt to «learn» Talmud.[11] It liked me, therefore, to send him forth to «learn» as he should, but I hardly knew where.

At that time Isaac Polack had a teacher in his house, a solid young man from Lissa [Poland] and a mighty Talmud scholar. This teacher heard that I wished to place my son out for his studies, and proposed I should give my boy in his care. He asked not a penny for board or teaching fees until the end of two years, at which time he promised to return me my son fit to expound Halacha and the Tosafists.[12]

I made inquiries after him, and everyone advised me to accept his offer. Whereat I drew up a contract with him, and sent my son in God's name with his teacher on to Lissa.

My son lost no time in writing me, first of his

safe arrival, and then, in truth weekly, of his great content with his teacher and of how earnestly he «learned.» And more of him I did not ask.

About two weeks later, my son Joseph wrote me, begging me to send on a half-year's payment for his board and teacher's fee. I was not, to be sure, obliged to do it—so he wrote me—but life had grown very dear in Lissa, so that his teacher was beset with the need of raising money, naturally a hindrance to the progress of the studies. But were his teacher relieved of these cares, he could the more rapidly advance in his learning. The teacher had other children from Hamburg—the letter continued—and their parents had all sent money, so he prayed me not to remain behind the others.

It really mattered little to me whether I paid the fees sooner or later, and I sent him the money for the half-year. So all went well, and I learned from passing travellers that my son worked hard at his studies.

But when the six months were nearly over, I received a letter from my son Joseph—it was on the eve of Sabbath as we made ready to go to synagogue —that read as follows:

> «My dear mother, you know that I have always been a good boy and never done anything against your wishes. So now I hope you will not withhold from me your mother's love, nor let me fall into the hands of the Gentiles.

«For I must tell you, mother dear, that the Jewish community of Lissa is greatly in debt to the church powers and cannot pay either capital or interest. The community sees no other way out, save to hand the children of the German Jews over to the church powers by way of a pledge. And then their German parents may ransom them as they can.

«The *parnas* of the community secretly revealed the plan to all the teachers with German pupils, and a Talmud student who is my good friend whispered it in my ears. I dare not write you of it myself, for my teacher watches me too closely and reads every one of my letters, so I have asked the young man to write in my stead.

«For the love of God, mother dear, write to Tockel's son-in-law to give me fifty or sixty Reichsthalers that I may pay my teacher and that he send me home in secrecy, and I escape from their hands.

«I beg you, in God's name, hasten! For if you delay I shall fall into the power, God forbid, of the Poles, and should that happen and it come to a question of ransom it will cost us tenfold. So I beg you, for a bit of money do not forsake your child, and let me not fall into hands from which it will be hard to get free.»

When I read this my strength left me. I summoned my son Mordecai and showed him the letter. He, too, was stricken with alarm. Sabbath had just begun. At its close we decided to send my son Mordecai to Lissa forthwith, and have him bring home my son Joseph.

Mordecai set out at once for Berlin, and thence to Frankfort-on-the-Oder. As he left the gate of Frankfort, my son Joseph came riding towards him in a little Polish cart. My son Mordecai saw him, bade him descend, and asked him by what strange hap he was riding to Frankfort and what he meant by such a letter to his mother. And he showed him the letter.

My son Joseph read it, and said, «What does it mean? Really, I haven't the slightest notion. My teacher—may his name be blotted out!—must have written it himself, and thought to pump another bit of money out of me, as he has already squeezed all he could and pleased. He has taken all my belongings, cut the silver buttons from my coat, and made off with everything.

«When I wanted to leave him, he charged me with all manner of false debts, I had eaten like a pig, devoured his house, and despoiled him. I saw that nothing good could come of it, so I asked Tockel's son-in-law to make terms with him. He paid thirty Reichsthalers and took me away, and sent me on here. Thank God I am free of that scoundrel! What is more, he taught me nothing.»

My son Mordecai was only too happy to have chanced on him, and they returned at once in their

coach to Hamburg. I rejoiced mightily and thereat
took me an honest teacher and had my son «learn»
at home.

8

About this time, something terrible happened in
Hamburg.

There lived in Altona one Abraham Metz, whose
wife was my kinswoman, Sarah the daughter of
Elias Cohen. Before coming to Hamburg he had
dwelt in Herford and married the daughter of
Loeb Herford. Two years after the marriage, his
wife died, whereat he moved to Hamburg and
took to himself the aforesaid Sarah.

He came a man of means, with some 3000
Reichsthalers or more; but strange to Hamburg, he
knew nothing of its ways or manners of business.
He kept losing ground steadily, and within a few
years he had nearly reached the end. Thereafter he
moved to Altona and became a money-changer.

One morning his wife comes to Hamburg and
asks of all the houses where he was known, if he
had not passed the night beneath their roof. But
despite all her inquiries she found no trace of him.
The woman now sank into despair. Many said she
had quarrelled with her husband and he had taken
to flight.

So the matter stood for three years, and everyone wagged their tongues as they pleased. There

were those who spoke great evil of him—God revenge his blood!—things that for the sake of a martyred saint I dare not repeat. But, alas for human frailty, our mouths often speak what our eyes have never seen.

Thus, for more than three years, our Sarah lived as a widow and sat with her fatherless children about her, suffering people to say and judge what they liked of her husband.

Then there was Aaron ben Moses,[13] another householder in Hamburg—a money-changer too, an honest man and by no means rich, yet a decent provider of his wife and children.

Now, money-changers must run about the whole day long in search of business, and towards afternoon prayers they return home and go to synagogue. Or they have every one his *chevra* [society] where they study Talmud and then betake themselves home.

One evening the wife of Reb Aaron waited till long after dark for her husband to return, that they might sup together. But she waited in vain. Then she ran out searching among all their friends, and found no sign of him. And he, too, remained lost.

The next day a cry went up everywhere. One man said he had seen him here, and another there.

When noon came, people gathered on the Bourse and talked of nothing else. Samuel, the son of

Meir Heckscher, said, «Yesterday a wench came to me, who had a little money. She asked me whether I had six or seven hundred thalers, and if so I should come home with her, where there was a well-to-do stranger who had quantities of gold and precious stones to sell. But I lacked the money and did not go with her.»

When he had finished his story, a man named Lipmann, who was standing by, asked him what kind of a person the wench might be, and how she was dressed. Whereat Samuel Heckscher told him. And Reb Lipmann said, «I know who she is, and where she works. And I have no reason to think good of her master.»

After this talk and more like it, everyone left the Bourse and went home.

When Reb Lipmann reached his house, he said to his wife, «What think you of this? The wench who works for the son of the keeper of the Navigators Tavern went up to Samuel Heckscher and wanted him, if he had six or seven hundred thalers about him, to go home with her. I fear me that the little fellow who is lost did as much, and it cost him his life.»

Then his wife struck her head and said, «By my sins! I remember now this wench once came to me, and wanted either you or me to go off with her. You know right well the wicked head that tavern-keeper's son carries on his neck. He is no one else but the murderer, and the little man, I say, was killed in his house.»

An energetic soul, the wife of Reb Lipmann swore she would give herself neither rest nor peace till she brought the matter to light. But her husband answered her, «Foolish woman, even if it were true, what could be done? This is Hamburg, and we dare not breathe a syllable about it.»[14]

Several days passed. Then the Town Council was induced to send forth a crier with a drum: whoso knew aught of the missing Jew, whether he be dead or alive, let him tell what he knew and he should receive a hundred ducats reward and his name would never be said.

But no one came with anything to tell.

So time went on, and the affair was nigh forgotten, as is the way of the world. No matter how urgent or important be a thing, if it leads nowhere, it soon vanishes from the mind of man. But not so the anguish of the grass-widow and her fatherless children.

9

Then, early of one Sabbath morning the wife of Reb Lipmann found she could not go to sleep.

Thus it was with the King of Spain who asked a learned Jew the meaning of the Hebrew words, *Hiné lo yonum ve-lo yishon shomer Yisroél.* Whereat the learned Jew gave him the plain mean-

ing, «Behold, He that keepeth Israel shall neither
slumber nor sleep.» But the King said, «Nay, it
means otherwise. Methinks it means «God, the
keeper of Israel, lets one neither slumber nor sleep.»
For had I slept this night as is my wont, the
slanders laid to the door of the Jews would have
brought them to their ruin. But God who is their
keeper would not let me sleep, and I rose and saw
the murdered child cast into the Jew's house. Had
I seen it not, it would have cost the life of all the
Jews.»[15]

So, too, the wife of Reb Lipmann could not sleep.
And early mornings she sat by her window, for she
lived in the top-storey on the Alter Steinweg
which leads to Altona, and everyone going to and
from Altona must pass her door.

That Friday night the poor woman never slept
a wink, and she drove everyone mad in the house.
Her husband groaned, what a life—she will drive
herself crazy! But she said, there was no help for
it, as long as the crime goes unavenged she could
give herself no peace, for well she knew and her
heart told her who had done the deed.

Meanwhile day broke, and she stood again at the
window and looked in the street. There she saw the
very man passing by with his wife, and a servant
went with them carrying a large chest.

When the woman saw them, she began to scream,
«God be with me now! And I'll have peace at

last!» And she snatched her apron and her shawl and ran down from the room.

Her husband sprang from the bed and sought to withhold her. But she shook herself loose and ran after the people.

They made their way to Altona and laid their chest by the bank of the Elbe. Rebecca—that was the name of Reb Lipmann's wife—was persuaded the chest held the body of the victim.

She flew to people in Altona and begged them, for God's sake, help her, for she knew she had the murderer before her eyes. But no one wanted to hearken to her, and they said, it is easy to begin something but who knows how it will end? However, she kept on crying, Only take me to the President!

Finally, two householders went with her to the President, and told him everything. Whereat the President said to them, «Beware of what you begin. If you do not prove what you say, all you have and hold is forfeit.»

But Frau Rebecca refused to be daunted, and said she would stake her very life upon it. «For the love of God,» she said, «send, my lord, and fetch the man and all he has with him.»

Then the President despatched watchmen and soldiers to the Elbe. The suspects had on the instant boarded ship heading for Harburg, about an hour away from Altona. Once they reached Harburg, they were free, for Harburg lay in another jurisdiction.

But the watch arrived in the nick of time, and brought the man, his wife and their chest back to the President. He ordered the chest opened. And naught was found save clothes that belonged to the man and his wife.

You can readily picture the alarm of the poor Jews. The man was questioned in every way, but he would own to nothing. On the contrary, he delivered himself of such threats that the Jews trembled with fear. For the man came of a very high family. And, finally, the Jews ran off in terror.

But Frau Rebecca never ceased saying, «Good folk, I beg you, do not despair—you will see how God shall help us!»

As she came running, all distraught, across the fields lying between Altona and Hamburg she met upon the wench who worked for the man. She knew the wench well, the same it was who had gone among the Jews to bring whosoever had six or seven hundred thalers to her master's house.

Frau Rebecca at once said to her, «Lucky for you and lucky for your master and mistress that we are met. Both of them are now imprisoned in Altona for the murder they have done. They have confessed to everything, and there lacks only your own confession, and once you have given it, the boat stands ready to carry you off to safety with your master and his wife. For all that the Jews want of you is to know that Reb Aaron be really dead, so his wife may be allowed to marry again. Apart from that we Jews want nothing from you.»

Frau Rebecca kept on talking to the wench in this strain. She was a clever and glib woman, and through her chatter she won the wench over into talking herself; and pell-mell the wench told everything: how she had met Reb Aaron on the Bourse, and later Reb Lipmann and other Jews, how none for a lucky lack of money went with her, save the poor Reb Aaron, cursed as he was with a full purse, and how she showed him a gold chain and told him that an officer in her master's house had gold and diamonds for sale.

«So this Aaron,» she continued, «went with me. But before he ever entered the house, the slaughter-block was set for him. My master led him down to his chamber, and we did away with him, and buried him under the threshold.»

And then she said, «Frau Rebecca, I have told you this in all confidence—you will not use it against me?» Whereat Frau Rebecca answered her, «Are you a fool? Don't you know my honest heart? I am thinking of naught but the safety of your master and mistress, that they go free from Altona. Once you come and tell our people what you have said, all will be well.»

So the maidservant went with Frau Rebecca to

the President's house. The President listened to the maid, and though she began to stammer and regret she had opened her mouth, still all was out, and not least the place where the victim lay buried.

Thereat the President summoned the murderer and his wife, each apart, and they both denied the deed, and said, «Everything our maid has told you is false, she lies like a strumpet.»

Once again this put a bad face on things, and the President said to the Jews, «I can help you no further. If I put the man to torture on the word of his maid, and he persists in his denials, 'twould be pretty work. It is for you to seek justice now in Hamburg, and quickly as you can. Secure leave from the authorities to search the house for the body, and should you find it as the maid has said, I shall see to the rest.»

The *parnassim* ran at once and arranged to bring twenty soldiers to the spot the maid had mentioned, and began digging. They also received leave, if the body were found, to carry it to Altona for a Jewish burial. But they were likewise warned, «Take you heed, if the body be not found, you are all of you done for. You know right well what sort the Hamburg rabble are—we could never hold them back.»

We one and all lay in grave danger. But Frau Rebecca was everywhere, at each man's elbow, and she kept repeating, «Do not weaken, I know in sooth the body will be found.» For the maidservant had talked away her life and given her no end of proof.

Ten stout-hearted fellows and a number of seamen known to be loyal and bold were gathered together, along with certain watchmen. And they went in God's name to the murderer's house, which lay not far from the Alten Schrangen, hard by the house of the jailer.

Meanwhile a cry arose throughout the city, and a mob of working-men and the general rout of *canaille*, countless numbers, swarmed before the door of the murderer's house.

With one will they said to themselves, «If the Jews find the body, well and good; but if they don't, there'll not be hide or hair left of them.»

But the good Lord did not keep us long in suspense. As soon as our people entered the house, they dug up the spot by the doorsill and found what they sought—at once with tears in their eyes and joy in their hearts.

They wept to find the youth of twenty-four in such a pitiable state, and rejoiced that the community was saved and justice at hand.

They summoned the entire Council, and showed them the body and the place where the maid said it would be found. The Council drew up a sworn statement of their findings and put their seal to the affidavit.

Then the body was placed on a cart and taken

to Altona. Throngs of seamen and apprentices looked on, I can't tell you how many, perhaps a hundred thousand; but not one of them let slip an evil word. Wicked folk though they were and even in peaceful times forever hounding the Jews, now they were silent, and each man returned quietly to his place.

The next day our *parnassim* took the affidavit and brought it to the President of Altona, who had the murderer and justice in his hands. And the Jews were better pleased to have the trial held in Altona.

The President again summoned the murderer and told him all that had passed. Whereat he confessed to everything. The widow received what share of the money still remained, and they sent the man back to prison for trial.

10

Meanwhile Frau Sarah, the wife of the vanished Abraham Metz, still passed as a grass-widow and could learn nothing of the whereabouts of her husband. Instead, she must endure, as I said, all manner of gossip.

But when the murder came to light and the murderer was on everyone's lips, it was recalled that before he lived in the house on the Alten Schrangen, he dwelt with his father in the Navigators, the finest tavern in all Hamburg. It lies hard by the

Bourse, and Jewish as well as Gentile merchants who have business on foot or accounts to reckon go therein, and drink together from silver cups.

The tavern-keeper's son was, therefore, well known among the Jews. When it came out that he was the murderer, people remembered that Frau Sarah's husband was a money-changer, and that all of his kind frequented the tavern and received or paid out money there in the course of their business—for it was an altogether honest and respectable house.

Frau Sarah also knew that her husband was well acquainted with the son of mine host. She went, then, and said to her friends: «You know how my husband vanished these years ago. And now this murder comes to light. My husband was forever going in and out of the tavern, and I verily believe the son has done away with him. Come to my aid, and perhaps we may learn that my husband likewise fell at his hands.»

To make a long story short, they went to the President and related what they had in mind. The President took the murderer and spoke him foul words and fair, and threatened him the rack, in the hope of wringing from him a confession. For a long while he would hear nothing of it, and only admitted that he knew our Abraham Metz.

But the President kept at him till he finally confessed that, while he was still living at his father's tavern, he had killed Reb Abraham in a little cheese-room, and thrust him there in a deep pit and covered the body with lime.

When this became known, the *parnassim* hastened again to the Town Council in Hamburg and begged leave to search the premises.

Again the Jews lay in danger, and even greater than before. That a highly honoured and respectable house should be an assassin's den! It would go hard with us were the body not to be found.

But fortune was with us. He still wore his red vest with silver buttons and his *arba kanfot* [ritual scarf]. And they drew him forth and brought him to a Jewish grave.

Our community fell into deep mourning, for it was as though both victims had lost their lives on the same day.

The friends of my kinswoman Frau Sarah carefully examined the body of the second victim before its burial. Frau Sarah had told them of sundry marks on the body whereby they could be certain it was the remains of her departed husband, and that she was in truth a widow. They found the marks and she became lawfully free to marry again.

The murderer was condemned to be broken on the wheel, and his body empaled and laden with irons, that he serve as an example for a long time to come. His wife and maid, however, were freed, and suffered no more than banishment.

The day of the execution proved more riotous than any known in Hamburg for a hundred years. The Jews stood in mortal danger, for a mighty hate rose against them.

But God, our Lord and Shepherd, who has ever in His mercy kept watch over us—as it is said, «When they be in the land of their enemies, I will not cast them away»[16]—did not forsake us on that day. If only we poor sinful creatures bethought us of the great wonders God works for us all our days!

So it all ended well for the Jews.

11

I will now resume from where I left off.

Several matches were proposed for my son Joseph, but none found favour with God save the daughter of Meir Stadthagen, who dwelt in Copenhagen. We, therefore, blessed the match and celebrated the betrothals in Hamburg. The wedding was set for a year later.

When time drew near for the wedding, which was to be held in Copenhagen, I planned to journey there with my son Nathan.

Nathan was now heavily engaged in business with the rich Samuel Oppenheimer of Vienna and his son Mendel. He held their notes to the amount of 20,000 Reichsthalers, and they were on the point of falling due. But my son received neither remittances whereby the notes might be met without default, nor even a letter explaining their delay. For this reason he found himself unable to go to Copenhagen. Instead, he must keep watch for his own honour and the honour of his correspondents.

You may readily conceive our worry and heart-ache. I set forth alone with my son Joseph, and God knows with what anxiety and bitterness of soul. For I knew naught of how things stood with the rich Viennese.

I left Hamburg together with the bridegroom and Moses, the son of Meir Stadthagen and the son-in-law of Chayim Cleve. And we arrived safe in Copenhagen.

There I awaited letters from my son Nathan, hoping to hear that he had received word and re-mittances from the wealthy Viennese. And in truth he wrote me, the good son he was, that though he had no news from Vienna I should not worry or rejoice any the less at the wedding.

Though my heart was not in it, still I left all in God's hands and dismissed my cares. We exchanged our dowries and the wedding was prepared for the following week.

From one post to another I awaited good news from my son Nathan. Praise be God, the tidings came the day before the wedding. Nathan wrote me that Mendel Oppenheimer had sent him remit-tances to several thousands more than were owing him or needed, together with apologies for the delay, due to his absence from Vienna. And the wedding was celebrated in high spirits and to our mutual content.

After the festivities I was anxious to speed my way home, but I had no other travelling companion than Moses, the son of Meir Stadthagen, and he was in no haste to leave his folks. So, against my will I remained two weeks in Copenhagen. Yet despite all the honours and courtesies they bestowed on me, I longed to be home with my little ones. At length I pressed Moses Stadthagen so hard, he consented to depart. Thereupon we set forth, and praise God, arrived safe and sound in Hamburg.

I went into accounting with my son Loeb for the wares I had left in his hands, and he gave me a clean bill for everything, so I was mighty content.

12

I still had four children in my house: my sons Samuel and Moses, and my daughters Freudchen and Miriam. Although many and excellent matches were proposed for my own person, so I might have once again become me honour and riches, I thought it against my children's wishes, and—to my misfortune as it will be seen—I refused every offer.

Meanwhile, my son Samuel had grown up, and from time to time I took him with me to the Brunswick Fair. He had no itch for studies, so I

thought best it to break him into business. My son
Moses, on the other hand, was a good student, and
I sent him to the Frankfort school to «learn» Talmud. And I sent with him my son Samuel with a
stock of goods.

While Samuel was trading in Frankfort, my
brother-in-law Joseph received a letter from his
good friend, the rich Moses Brillin of Bamberg,
asking advice with regard to a Hamburg match
proposed for his daughter.

The letter reached my brother-in-law on a Sabbath, and he called me at once to his house. I
found him walking in the garden with my sister
Elkele.

When I appeared he cried out to me, «Mazel tov
[congratulations]— your son Samuel is betrothed!»
I laughed and said, «If so, I ought to know of it.»

Whereat he showed me the letter from Moses
Bamberg who was then in Vienna, and another
from the right learned Chief Rabbi Samson Wertheimer[17] of Vienna, likewise writing him for his
honest advice as to the proposed match.

I read the letter and said to my brother-in-law,
«Still I can't see that my son Samuel is betrothed.»
And he answered, «I guarantee, once I have answered these letters, your son will be engaged to
the daughter of Moses Bamberg.»

The right learned Chief Rabbi Samson was, you
must know, the brother-in-law of Moses Bamberg,

and Joseph wrote him at once of my son Samuel. The match was born of the two letters, and the Chief Rabbi Samson wrote for my son to come directly to Vienna and remain with him until the wedding—which was set for two years later.

It is not to be told, the magnificent promises that the right learned Chief Rabbi Samson showered on me—he wrote me, «God did send me before you to preserve life»[18]—assuring me all would be well with my son Samuel and his brothers. And I received many letters thereafter from the princely rich Rabbi Samson breathing the warmest friendship.

My son Samuel was, as I said, at the Frankfort Fair. I wrote him of his betrothal and bade him, at the close of the fair, set forth to Vienna and remain there until the wedding.

The learned and rich Rabbi Samson received him with honours and had him write me of his content, and that a teacher had been procured for him. But my son Samuel was still very young, and gave himself over to childish follies. And Rabbi Samson gave little heed to him. So within the two years he had squandered a large sum of money.

My son, to be sure, wrote me everything and urged me to hasten the marriage, for he had no desire to linger in Vienna. But as his bride was young and tiny, the wedding was postponed for nearly another year.

The father-in-law, Moses Bamberg, was likewise

in Vienna, and at my repeated letters, consented that the nuptials take place in Bamberg on the first of Tamuz. My son Samuel wrote me he would set forth with his prospective father-in-law, and I should order my affairs so as to be in Bamberg at the set date.

Since I was attending the Leipzig Fair in any case, I planned to proceed thence to Bamberg.

Then it was, the rich Chief Rabbi Samson wrote me that, because of the rage against the Jews in Hamburg, I had best come to Vienna immediately after the wedding and dwell in his house. He offered me two of his best rooms and bade me engage in any business I would, and to this end sent me a puissant Imperial passport. I arranged my affairs accordingly and never doubted that I should move to Vienna. I converted 50,000 Reichsthalers into jewellery, which I thought to take with me to my new home. But «there are many devices in a man's heart; nevertheless the counsel of the Lord, that shall stand.»[19]

So I set forth to Leipzig with my son Nathan and my boy Moses. On our arrival my son Nathan received letters from Hamburg bidding him, upon the close of the fair, return home for business reasons. Whereat my departure for Vienna suffered postponement, for I had no will to journey there without my son Nathan.

I sent my jewellery back with him to Hamburg,

keeping only some few thousands' worth in hand, and set forth towards Bamberg, alone with my boy Moses. The journey was beset with hardships, for the road was far from safe, and a lone woman, I had no one at my side save my fifteen-year-old son. Still, with money all roads can be travelled—but it cost me a mighty sum.

I arrived at Bamberg towards midnight. The next morning, the bride and her parents welcomed me. I had thought, as you know, that the wedding would be held forthwith, on the first day of Tamuz.

But a great rumpus intervened. Without my knowledge, my brother-in-law Joseph had written into the betrothal-contract the sum of 5000 thalers for the bridegroom's dowry, whereas my son had no more than 4000 thalers.

We were already aware of this in Hamburg, and I had written on the spot to Samson Wertheimer that the 5000 thalers was an error, and that my son possessed but 4000 thalers in German money. He had answered me it mattered nothing, we should let the contract stand, it only heightened the honour thereof, and no word of it would be breathed at the wedding.

But now Moses Bamberg spoke in a different strain; he would hear of nothing but the terms of the contract. We had such a falling-out that the wedding could not be held on the agreed date.

Moses Bamberg wrote at once to Vienna, and Samson Wertheimer answered no more than the truth. Meanwhile, e'er the answer came, Moses Bamberg sought to squeeze out of me what he could. But when he saw there was nothing to be squeezed, and the letter from Vienna gave me right, the wedding took place toward the middle of Tamuz—with all the splendour and honours we Jews could provide.

Many eminent Jews of the province were in attendance. Among them, two sons of the rich Samson Baiersdorf[20] who brought with them a marriage broker.

There had already been a proposal in Hamburg for my son Moses and the daughter of Samson Baiersdorf. Since Baiersdorf lay only fifteen miles from Bamberg, I had promised the Hamburg broker, once the wedding was over, to take my son to Baiersdorf, to see and be seen.

The two sons of the rich Samson Baiersdorf, who were both married, now spoke to me and told me what dowry I might expect. For answer, I told them that after the wedding we were taking a pleasure excursion to Fürth, not more than ten miles from Baiersdorf. And then we should know what to do. For my son had received proposals both in Bamberg and in Fürth.

So I agreed with the rich Moses Bamberg, the father-in-law of my son Samuel, that we make a

Bride and Groom Beneath the Wedding Canopy
In the Synagogue Courtyard—Fürth

common excursion to Fürth. We had already looked into the Bamberg match, and now proposed to do as much in Fürth and Baiersdorf.

Moses Bamberg and his wife, and I and my son Moses, now set out on our pleasure jaunt. We visited Baiersdorf and saw the daughter of Reb Samson. He likewise saw my son, and the match was within an ace of being clinched—only a matter of a thousand thalers stood between us.

Then we journeyed on to Fürth and remained there overnight. I cannot begin to tell you of the honours heaped upon us. The most eminent Jews of the community, together with their wives, descended on our inn and made to carry us off to their homes. In the end we could not resist a kinsman of the son of my cousin Mordecai Cohen, and must go with him. That evening we were handsomely entertained in his home.

The next morning we left Fürth without concluding aught with respect to the match. And when I reached Bamberg I set about making preparations to return home with my son Moses.

But the marriage broker who had urged the Baiersdorf match, though he lived in Fürth, never seemed to leave Bamberg and showed himself mighty eager to conclude the betrothals. But I let him know my resolution in no uncertain words: thus and so it must be, and no otherwise.

Finally the broker said: «I plainly see you'll have

no other terms and that you are set upon your departure. Yet do me but the favour to tarry until two this afternoon. I have written them everything in Baiersdorf, and I'm certain we shall hear before two o'clock that all is in order. But if by two no answer comes, I'll detain you no longer.»

I was content, and meanwhile finished my packing. My son Samuel and his father-in-law, the rich Moses Bamberg, proposed to do us the honour of accompanying us for several miles.

Meanwhile a dinner was served like a banquet in the days of King Solomon. I cannot tell you what a good and wise man is Moses Bamberg and the honour he does to men.

When we had eaten and drunk our fill, the hour had already struck three. And from Baiersdorf nothing was seen or heard. So we set out, the whole company of us, and left Bamberg towards five o'clock. Although Moses Bamberg had urged me, since night was approaching, to remain over until next morning, I was set against it, and we journeyed forth in God's name.

We were barely a quarter-hour beyond the city when the marriage broker, *nebbich*, comes riding after us and begs us by all that is holy to return to Bamberg. The sons of Samson Baiersdorf, he said, were there and willing to meet my terms. But I was determined not to turn back.

Moses Bamberg thereupon said to me, «Look

you, there lies a pretty village before us, with a comfortable inn. Night is most fallen, and we shall be able to proceed but little farther. Let us pass the night in the inn, and if Samson Baiersdorf's sons wish to come to us, well and good.»

I was content and the marriage broker happy. Having at least brought us to a halt, he wheeled about and sped back to Bamberg. Not an hour had passed when an imposing company drew up at the inn: Rabbi Mendel Rothschild of Bamberg, the two sons of Samson Baiersdorf, Loeb Biber of Bamberg and his brother Wolf, all of them distinguished and eminently rich people.

To put it in brief, there was little discussion, and the betrothals were brought to a happy conclusion. The two sons were given full powers by their father, and they signed everything. And we passed the evening in great merriment and joy.

The rich Samson Baiersdorf was not at home at the time, but in Bayreuth attending on His Highness the Margrave, with whom he stood in high esteem—he was, as everyone knows, his court Jew.[21] His sons begged us to do them the favour and their father the honour of visiting them in Bayreuth.

This seemed at first blush very difficult, for we had engaged our coach as far as Halberstadt. But we talked to the driver and finally agreed with him to pay two thalers more to take us by way of Bayreuth, and thence by way of Naumburg where a fair was in full swing. Seckel Wiener, who was likewise with us, approved of the plan.

Whereat Moses Bamberg said to me that if it would render me a friendly service he would be only too happy to accompany me to Bayreuth. I refused his tender with many polite compliments, and would not hear of imposing on him so heavy a burden. Still, it came about in the end that the whole company of us set out for Bayreuth.

There we met the rich and mighty Samson Baiersdorf who heartily rejoiced in our coming. The month of Ab, it is true, had already begun and somewhat dampened our joy—that very evening we were served but a meagre supper, for there was little to be had.[22]

But next day Samson Baiersdorf sent porters scurrying out for all sorts of excellent fish, and he had prepared whatever other *milchige* [meatless] dishes could be hastily got together, for I could hold out no longer. My new kinsman promised me I should not have to hold out later than one o'clock.

And so, after dining, we bade one another farewell, and I and my betrothed son Moses, together with Seckel Wiener, placed ourselves in the coach, and we parted truly in tears from Moses Bamberg.

We reached Hamburg in safety, and after twelve weeks' absence found my children and all the family, praise God, in excellent health.

13

Some time later, God visited upon my cousin Bela (the wife of the wealthy and learned Baer Cohen) a peculiar sickness—may we never know it!—so that she could not pass water, and thus it was for four long weeks.

The rich Baer Cohen brought every well-tried means to bear, and no end of physicians, and emptied his purse to ransack the world for all possible physicking and curative devices, but, alas, in vain. God, it seemed, had passed His decree. And so her torments endured.

When at last my kinswoman Bela saw that she worsened every day, and that all cures had failed, she took for witness my brother-in-law Joseph and Rabbi Samuel Orgels, and summoned her husband, and spoke feelingly with him in behalf of her orphaned niece Glückchen, whom she had raised in her own house and who was now eleven or twelve years old. Both of them loved the child dearly.

Frau Bela begged her husband for the peace of her soul to assure her, e'er she died, and give his hand upon it, he would remarry no one else save her orphaned niece Glückchen, the daughter of the departed Feibisch Cohen. Whereat Baer Cohen promised with streaming eyes. He gave his hand to my brother-in-law and to Rabbi Orgels, and solemnly pledged his word. And his wife set herself at peace, and said she was content to die, knowing she had provided for her Glückchen. But, God knows! things come not always to pass as we mortals think.

They wrote to Glückchen's brother Selig in Hanover, whom they had likewise reared and married to the daughter of the rich Hirz Hannover, and bade him come to his aunt who lay mortally sick and wished to see him before she died.

Meanwhile the remedies had done their work, and many vessels of water passed from her, and they thought it foretold her recovery. But, alas, it only hastened the end. When her nephew Selig reached her side, he found her seemingly better, but before the day had passed God took her away, to the great grief of her husband and all our friends and the entire community.

She was, God be gracious to her! a woman of valour and wisdom, who knew how to rule the heart of her husband. But what did it all avail her? All her money and goods and everything her husband had done for her proved of no aid. He set scholars to «learn» for her and lavished gifts of mercy, but, so it seemed, her time had come, and at the last New Year prayer of «who will live and who will die» her term was sealed.

She died in all honour and was carried to her grave. Her husband and her friends mourned her deeply, above all my kinsman Anschel Wimpfen, his wife Mata—a niece of the departed—and Mata's brother Reuben, likewise reared in the house of Baer Cohen. Mata and Reuben were cousins of the orphan Glückchen.

They took comfort somewhat, after the seven days of mourning, in the thought that Baer Cohen's houses would not be estranged from them, forasmuch as it would be the home of their near kinswoman Glückchen.

They at once began to press Baer Cohen to publish his intention of wedding their cousin Glückchen and give himself peace from the marriage brokers. Of a truth the brokers allowed him no rest, for every father with a daughter on his hands, if only he could muster up the means, would have liked nothing better than an alliance with the rich and learned Baer Cohen.

From time to time Baer Cohen reassured the kin of Glückchen, but urged the moment was too soon. But finally, it came out: the marriage was impossible, he had reared Glückchen as his own child under his own roof and had ever looked on her as his daughter. Moreover, he was a childless man and no longer young. How, then, take unto himself a wife who for some years at least could not bear him children? And if he choose to wait until she came of age to do so, who knows whether he would still be alive, or being so would not fulfil his pledge?

This talk and its like badly frightened all her

friends. They touched his heart with the recollection that he had given his hand to witnesses and pledged his wife on her death-bed to marry little Glückchen.

Whereupon he answered them. «It is all true,» he said, «but I gave my word in order to content my wife. Moreover, I was so distraught at the time I did not know what I was saying. I beg you, prevail on Glückchen to release me from my promise, and I will give her a dowry that will bring her as fine a husband as myself. But if you fear that my house will thereby become estranged to you, tell me of another marriageable maiden in your family and I will take her to wife and still do what I have said for Glückchen.»

But Reb Anschel and Frau Mata and her brother Reuben Rothschild favored Glückchen and none else. Perhaps they felt that in another marriage, even with one of their own kin, they would lose their place in Baer Cohen's house. For at that time they held great sway, and at their word all in the house «came and went.»[23]

My daughter Freudchen was now only twelve, but she was a big girl for her years and lovely beyond compare. Whereat my brother Wolf came to me and said, «Why do you sit in idleness? Baer Cohen is not marrying Glückchen—I shall propose to him your daughter Freudchen.» I laughed at my brother and scolded him as well. «What talk is this?» I said. «Shall I come between an orphan child and her marriage?»

But my brother swore he knew for a surety that Baer Cohen would not marry Glückchen, and if not my daughter, he will take an outsider and the whole family will be estranged from his house. Now who, indeed, would not gladly ally himself with Baer Cohen, a man of every excellence in the world!

So, presently, my brother went to Baer Cohen and proposed the match. He answered that in truth he did not know my daughter, but let the proposal be discussed with Anschel Wimpfen, his wife Mata, and her brother Reuben. If they can be induced to prevail on Glückchen to release him, for himself he was content. However, when my brother spoke to them, they fell into a rage, and Frau Mata as much as said, «Before I let him take Freudchen Hameln, I'd rather see him marry a rank outsider.» When I heard of this, I gave no further regard to the match.

Meanwhile Baer Cohen talked with Glückchen and besought her to free him from his word. He offered her a princely dowry and any excellent young man she pleased. But she would not hear of it.

Thereupon he wrote to several rabbis, laying before them the circumstances and begging permission to take another woman to wife. The very

learned rabbi of the Talmud school of Altona refused consent, but, it is said, other rabbis granted
his request.

For all his desire to have Baer Cohen marry
Glückchen, Anschel Wimpfen now saw that further steps were useless. Baer Cohen, it appears, had
long set his heart on wedding the daughter of
Tevele Schiff. And he presently did so. Within a
year she bore him a young son, and you can picture
his joy.

However, shortly before this, Anschel Wimpfen
died suddenly. He went to bed in the best of
health, but before he was in bed an hour he
breathed his pure soul away. He was mourned by
the whole community, for he was an excellent,
God-fearing man.[24]

While I was at the Leipzig Fair about a year and
a half after Baer Cohen's second marriage, the news
came of the serious illness of his wife, and with the
next post the tidings she was dead. Not long thereafter he married her sister.

Rabbi Samuel Orgels had his hand in all these
affairs and stood high in the esteem of Baer Cohen.
And it was not long e'er, one Friday evening in
synagogue, Rabbi Orgels fell into a faint and died
on the spot.

You can imagine for yourselves the alarm of the
community. Within a short space Anschel Wimp-

fen, Rabbi Samuel Orgels, and the second wife of Baer Cohen had laid themselves down and died.

Whether my kinswoman Bela had ought to do with the death of the two witnesses to the broken pledge God alone knows. I and all mortal men are too weak to judge of such things. We can only pray to God Almighty, praised be His name! that He turn away His wrath from us and from all Israel.

In the end Baer Cohen married off his niece to excellent advantage. He gave her to the son of the rich Judah Berlin, and did nobly by her brothers and sisters, as the wide world knows.

The whole story has no place in my book, and I only told it to show the fickleness of human fate.

Before her death, my cousin Bela thought she had climbed to the highest rung of human happiness, as indeed she had by all mortal account. She had for husband Baer Cohen, a great Talmud scholar, a scion of the priestly tribe and of a good family, a conspicuously rich, great-hearted and benevolent man. They lived together happily, and though childless, she had by her side Glückchen and Selig, the children of Feibisch Cohen, whom she raised as though they were her own. Her sole care was for the well-being of these children, and she lived to see Selig betrothed to the daughter of the rich Hirz Hannover. I have heard her say with her own lips that the youth cost her over 15,000

Reichsthalers, and she did as much by his sister. When he was betrothed after her heart's desire, her joy was beyond words. At that time she stood in higher regard and honour than any woman in all Germany.

But, alas, when the cord is stretched to its full, it breaks. In her best years and at the peak of her happiness she needs must go. And when in the throes of death she still thought to have her will, it came to pass otherwise.

What, then, availed her all her wealth and honours? «There is no man hath power in the day of death.»[25] Her true humbleness of spirit and the great good she did will abide by her; but they alone remain of all her riches.

She was about fifty-one years of age. She brought little money to her marriage, not nine hundred thalers all told, and the Most High had blessed her as everyone has seen.

God gave Baer Cohen vast wealth and posterity as well, which the Lord preserve until the Messiah come! The Lord enlarged his borders, for Baer Cohen was a big-hearted man and you will rarely see the like of him.

Here we might well apply a passage I found in the book *Yesh Nochalin*[26] with commentaries by the learned Rabbi Isaiah Hurwitz, which I had read to me in German. It is filled with admonitions and other like matters that roll on the tongue like honey, and whoever wishes to learn more of it may read the aforesaid book.

Dear children, fear God with all your heart. What you do not receive in this world, God will bestow upon you manyfold in the world to come, if only you will serve Him with all your soul and might—as I have so often told you and mean to tell you no more.

14

I will now return to my subject.

Somewhile thereafter I betrothed my daughter Freudchen to the son of the rich and eminent Moses ben Loeb.[27]

Meanwhile we were threatened with another blow, which God averted in His mercy. My son Nathan was, as I said, heavily engaged in business with the princely Samuel Oppenheimer of Vienna and his son Mendel. And again he held their notes which were about to fall due. My son, as you know, was accustomed to receive their remittances in time to meet the notes. But now neither remittances nor any word from them came to hand.

At last the sad tidings reached us that Samuel Oppenheimer and his son were flung into prison.[28] As fast as the news spread through Hamburg my son's credit was lost, and whoever held a note in his hands, whether of Oppenheimer or another, pressed my son for instant payment.

So my son had flung at his neck scores of notes, and others followed fast, none of which he dared protest or refuse to honour. The Leipzig Fair was now opening, which he needs must attend. Whereat he paid what he could, pawning all his gold and silver plate, and set out for Leipzig with a heavy heart.

When he parted from me, he said, «Mother dear, I am taking leave of you and God knows how it will be when we meet again. I still have many thousands to pay. Help me, I beg of you, so far as you can—I know the Oppenheimers will not leave me stranded.»

My son Nathan rode off with his party of travellers on a Sunday. And Monday my troubles began with the payment of the notes. I did what I could, mortgaged all I had, and went over my head in debt, till I could go no further. When Friday came I still had 500 thalers to pay, but no means of raising it.

I still possessed bills on a prominent house in Hamburg, which I thought to sell on the Bourse; and I wearily went the rounds of the Bourse, giving them into the brokers' hands. But when the exchange was closed, the brokers brought me back my bills, for no one wished to accept them.

I was in sore distress, but at length God enabled me somehow to pay the 500 thalers.

On Sabbath I resolved to go to Leipzig, and if

I found that the Oppenheimers had sent their remittances to the fair, I would return at once to Hamburg. Otherwise, I determined to go from Leipzig straight to my faithful friend Samson Wertheimer in Vienna, who would surely aid us to regain possession of our own.

I asked my brother Wolf to accompany me. We set forth in a hired wagon, and shortly before reaching Leipzig I halted at a village. Thence I despatched a messenger to my children in the city, bidding them come to me at once.

They came and told me that the great and rich Oppenheimers were set free, and had sent on remittances to cover all the notes. Quick as I heard this, I sat myself again in the wagon, we wheeled about, and before the Sabbath began I was back in Hamburg. Thus I spent six days to and fro on the road between Hamburg and Leipzig.

Shall I try to tell you the great joy of my children, poor things, above all the joy of my daughter-in-law Miriam, the wife of my son Nathan? We had parted in such distress we never thought to meet again so simply. But God—praise and thanks to the Most High!—had truly helped us in a twinkle.

Even though the rich Oppenheimers paid us for all we had laid out, they could never in all their days repay us for the terror and distress we suffered. May the ever-blessed God continue His mercies toward us and give us to eat our daily bread!

So, praise God all ended well.

15

My daughter Freudchen then married the son of Moses ben Loeb Altona. The wedding was beautifully celebrated in Altona, and with all joy.

Meanwhile the wedding of my son Moses drew nigh, and I wrote to Samson Baiersdorf I was all ready to depart. But he replied that it was impossible to hold the wedding at the agreed date. For since God had given him the grace to see his youngest child married, he meant to celebrate the occasion in a new and worthy house. He had set himself to building one, and as soon as it was finished, he would write me to come and solemnize the wedding in befitting pomp and honours.

However, the building of the house was not the chief or only reason. His Highness the Margrave in Bayreuth had taken to himself a new Counsellor who played the Haman to Samson Baiersdorf and sought to destroy him. In truth he pressed Samson Baiersdorf so hard, he knew not where to turn, the more so since the Margrave had possession of all his goods.

But the ever-blessed God who saw, nevertheless, all the good he had done, with what open arms he received both rich and poor, and how he came to the aid of all the Jews in the land, and that he truly kept the whole land together and could do as much or more in the future—in His grace and mercy God cast down the wicked Haman and turned all his evil into good, so that the wicked were overthrown and Samson Baiersdorf rose higher every day. It cannot be told in what esteem the princes held this Jew. May the Father of goodness preserve him till the day of redemption!

It was a full year before we could celebrate the marriage.

And I will now close my fifth book.

THE END OF MY FIFTH BOOK

BOOK SIX

1

IN THIS sixth book I will tell of the change in my life which I had sought to avoid these fourteen long years.[1]

Many matches were offered me during this time, among them truly the most eminent in all Germany. But as long as I was able, and as long as I felt I could support myself with what my blessed husband left me, the thought of remarriage never once entered my mind.

Doubtless the Most High saw my manifold sins and never gave me the thought to take to myself a husband when matches were proposed to me that would have rendered my children happy and provided me, not with my present anxious care-ridden old age, but a calm and sheltered life. But the Most High pleased otherwise, and because of my sins He allowed me to resolve upon the match I will now put before you.

Nevertheless, I thank my Creator for showing me more mercy and grace in my heavy punishment than I, unworthy sinner, merit or deserve, and for teaching me patience with all my sorrows.

I ought to witness my thanks, I know, in heavy fasts and other penitence, but my many cares and my sojourn in a strange land have kept me from doing as I should. I know that these excuses will help me little in the sight of God. I write this, therefore, with trembling hands and hot bitter tears, for it says that we shall serve the Lord with all our heart and all our might. It behooves us sinners, then, to spare neither our body nor our worldly means in the service of God, and all our self-justification is idle vanity.

I pray God Almighty to strengthen me in His mercy, and give me no thought save to serve Him faithfully, that I come not before Him in my stained garments—as it is said, «Repent the day before thy death,» but man knows not on what day he may die, therefore, let him repent every day of his life.[2]

So should I have done, and well I had the means to do it. But I made myself the poor excuse, first I will marry off my fatherless children, and then I will betake me to the Holy Land. And I could have done it very well, above all after my son Moses was betrothed and there only remained my youngest daughter Miriam. Aye, sinner that I am, I should have married off my Miriam and giving no thought to a second marriage done what beseems a good, pious Jewish woman: leaving behind me all the nothingness of this world, I should have taken myself, with the handful that remained me, to the Land of Our Fathers. There I might have lived as a good Jewess, and the cares and griefs of my children and all the other vanities of the world would no longer have burdened me, and there I might have served God with all my heart and soul. But my sins brought it to pass that God led me to other thoughts, and held me unworthy of it.

2

Now I will resume my tale.

A whole year passed before the marriage of my son Moses fell due. Meanwhile reverses and troubles, falling partly to the lot of my children, overwhelmed me, and before and as always cost me great sums of money. But there is little need to write of it. They were my children and I forgive them all, both those who cost me much and those who cost me naught, for bringing me to my straitened circumstances.

Moreover, I was still harassed by a large business, for my credit had not suffered among either Jews or Gentiles, and I never ceased to scrape and scurry. In the heat of summer and the rain and snow of winter I betook me to the fairs, and all day long I stood in my store.

Yet so little remained to me of all I once had, the

outlook soured upon me, and I put forth desperate efforts to maintain my footing and not fall a burden on my children and eat the bread of another. Though it would have meant my children's bread, it seemed bitterer than the bread of strangers, for my children, God forbid, might have cast it in my teeth, and the thought of this was worse than death.

Despite all my pains and travelling about and running from one end of the city to another, I found I could hold out no longer. For though I had a good business and enjoyed large credit, I stood in constant torment, once let a bale of goods go astray or a debtor fail me, I might fall, God forbid, into complete bankruptcy and be compelled to give my creditors all I had, a shame for my children and my pious husband asleep in the earth.

Then it was I began to regret the many marriages I might have made, bringing me riches and honour in my old age, and perhaps to the benefit of my children as well. But my regrets were in vain. It was too late. God had not willed it, and now He led my thoughts to where disaster lay in wait for me.

We were in the year of Creation 5459 [1698-99]. My son Moses, as I said, was awaiting his marriage. And then a letter came from my son-in-law Moses Krumbach in Metz, dated the 15th of Sivan [June, 1699]. He wrote me that Hirz

Lévy[3] had lost his wife, that he was an excellent
Jew, conspicuous for his learning and wealth, and
maintained a princely house—in short, he mightily
praised him, and apparently with truth. But «man
looketh on the outward appearance, but the Lord
looketh on the heart.»[4]

The letter reached me in the full tide of my distress. I was then a woman of fifty-four and had
consumed my life with the cares of my children.
If all I read were true, I could still pass my last
years in a pious community, for Metz had the name
of such in those days, and live out my days in
peace, and do somewhat too for the good of my
soul. I also depended upon my children to advise
me against it, if it were not to my interests.

And I wrote my son-in-law for answer: I had
been a widow for fourteen years and never bethought me to take another husband, though, as
everyone knew, I could have made the most bril-
liant marriage in all Germany. But now at his
earnest behest, I would give my consent providing
that his wife, my daughter Esther, shared his mind.

Thereupon my daughter Esther wrote me what
she saw and knew, much in the strain of her husband.

There was little discussion with respect to the
dowry. I gave my husband truly all I had, and he
assured me in writing that, were I to die first, my
heirs should have my money back again. But were

he to die before me, I was to receive 500 thalers more than I had brought him—which had been 1500 Reichsthalers. My husband likewise undertook to rear my daughter Miriam, then a child of eleven, at his own cost until her marriage.

Had I possessed more money, still I would have given it to him, for I believed it could not have been in surer hands. Moreover, I thought I had done well by my daughter Miriam; she need spend nothing of her own, and meanwhile her money lay out at interest. Besides, my husband had a great talent for business, and who knows what I still might earn for my children?

3

Alas, «there are many devices in a man's heart» but «He that sitteth in the heavens shall laugh at them.»[5] The Most High God laughed at my plans and proposals; He had long before decreed my ruin and disaster, to punish me for the sin of placing my reliance in my fellow-men. For I ought not to have thought of taking another husband. I could never find a second Chayim Hameln, and better had it been for me to remain by my children, accepting good and evil with what grace I could, as God meant it.

But these things are all over and done, and we cannot change the past. All that remains me is to pray God I hear and see nothing but good of my children. As for myself, I willingly take from the hand of God whatever be my portion. May the great and righteous King only give me patience as before, and count it all as an atonement for my sins!

The betrothals were concluded in the deepest secrecy. I did not wish them known because of the high tax due to the Town Council on departing for good from the city. It would have cost me several hundred thalers, for I was well known in Hamburg, and every merchant who dealt with me thought I was worth many thousands. Meanwhile I converted my goods into money and paid my debts, so that, praise and thanks to God, when I left Hamburg I owed no man, Jew or Gentile, a single thaler.

My children, my brothers and sisters, and all my close friends knew of the marriage. Yet even though I had taken counsel with them and they had all approved of it, still it went awry. «For the thing which I greatly feared is come upon me.»[6]

When I consented to the match I feared that were I to remain struggling as I was, I should lose all I had and, God forbid, suffer the shame of harming others, both Jews and Gentiles, and finally fall to the care of my children. But, alas, I was to fall into the care of a husband, and suffer the very shame I feared.

Helpless though I be, he is still my husband, with

whom I thought to live in ease and plenty. And now I find myself in such a state, I wonder whether I shall have a roof above my hoary head or a crumb of bread to eat. And my children whom I thought to spare the burden may yet be at pains to take me in.

I believed I was marrying a man who with his means and distinguished station could have aided my children and put them in the way of great wealth. But the very contrary happened. My son Nathan lost the many hundreds my husband owed him, and it brought him near to ruin. His notes would all have gone defaulted had not God, praised be His Name, come plainly to his aid. And my little daughter Miriam—I thought I had done so well by her in placing her money at interest with my husband. And I had brought her down in our common ruin, save that God, as you will learn, turned the blow from her young head.

Thus you see, my dear children, I had considered all, and meant and held for good the very things that proved the greatest evils. I cannot help but think my sins had found me out.

And so, beloved children of my heart, what more can I write? «There is no new thing under the sun.»[7] It has happened not only to me but to many others, better and godlier folk than I, and in whose footsteps I am not worthy to tread—as you may learn from the following story, which is for certain a true story and one that happened. If, dear children, you are wise and hearken closely, you must needs agree that the story is true.

Since the world nowadays likes a new story, I have written it from the Hebrew into German.

4

The story of a king who lived in Araby: Once upon a time there was a mighty king named Jedijah. He had many wives and many more sons and daughters. But his best-beloved son was Abadon, a handsome but a wild, hot-spirited youth.

Now Abadon had a sister Danila, and she was so beautiful everyone called her the Fair Danila. And it came to pass that one of her many half-brothers, a young man named Emunis, fell desperately in love with her, yet for fear of his father dared not possess her.

He finally confessed to a friend that he was poisoned by the beauty of Fair Danila, and begged the friend advise him how he might be cured. The friend bade him pretend he was deathly sick, as indeed he gave every appearance of being, and when his father King Jedijah came to visit his bedside, he must tell him he could eat no food, and beg the king send Fair Danila to his room, and perchance if she prepared a dish with her own hands, it might be possible for him to eat of it. And once the maiden was by him, he could do as he would with her. Moreover, his mother, who was a favourite of the king, might easily appease his father's wrath.

So it came to pass, and when the maiden had prepared the dish for Emunis, he said to her, «Sister dear, bring me the food to my bed, for if I eat it from your hand it will taste the better.» And when she brought the dish to his side, he seized hold of her and said, «You must lie with me, or else I die.» And despite all her protests he worked his will upon her.

But as soon as he had done so, all his love for her turned to hate and he drove her crying from the room. Still weeping, she met her brother Abadon and told him what had happened. And Abadon bade her stay in his house till he had wreaked his vengeance on his half-brother Emunis.

A little later Abadon managed to fall upon Emunis and kill him. Whereat the king, upon the evil counsel of Emunis' friends, drove his favourite son Abadon into banishment.

It was not many years before Abadon returned at the head of an army, drove his father from his capital city, lay waste his father's palace and put his wives and concubines to spoil. But in a final battle Abadon was killed. And the king, after his many misfortunes, regained his throne and ruled gloriously to the end of his days.

So, my children, you may see that though each

man meant well enough, his good intentions brought him to folly, and he was paid in accordance with his folly. Emunis meant to cure himself of love, but he listened to a fool's advice and his love turned to hate and he died for his hate. Abadon meant only to revenge his sister but he was led to overthrow and shame his father, and for that he died. The king Jedijah meant nothing more than to correct his beloved son, but in doing so he condoned the crime of Emunis and thereby lived to see his city spoiled, his throne lost, and his wives and concubines dishonoured.

5

I will now return to my subject.

The betrothals were concluded in Sivan, 5459 [June, 1699], at Metz, through the hand of my son-in-law Moses Krumbach and his father and mother. I am assured they meant it only for the best, and thought I had done well by myself, and so indeed it seemed. The wedding was set for Lagbeomar, 5460 [May 7, 1700], but it was all kept quiet for the reasons I have given.

Meanwhile I sent what money remained me to the rich Gabriel Levi of Fürth, in the form of bills of exchange, and bade him keep them till my arrival.

During this time I corresponded with my prospective husband, and he so worded his letters that

I and all who read them received naught but the most reassuring impressions and foresaw nothing of the disaster to which I was being led.

It was about Tebet, 5460 [January, 1700], that I decided to stop at Baiersdorf on my way, and after celebrating the wedding there of my son Moses, proceed forthwith to Metz.

But God visited me with a sickness that kept me to my bed for six weeks. My future husband learned of it through a merchant, and it cannot be told the consoling letters he wrote both to me and to my brother-in-law Joseph, and how he bade me take care of myself. God alone knows what his intentions were. If it were for the bit of money I had, I shall never discover.

As soon as, with God's help, I regained my full strength, I journeyed from Hamburg to Brunswick in the company of my son Moses and my youngest daughter Miriam. The fair was in swing, and I sold what was left of my wares.

After the fair, I travelled in good company, together with my children, as far as Bamberg, where I remained over the Feast of Purim. Then we set forth, together now with my son Samuel, for Baiersdorf where I expected to celebrate my son's wedding on the 1st of Nisan [April].

We put up at an inn across the way from Samson Baiersdorf, for his new house was still unfinished, and his old one too small. However, we ate with him three times a day, and were entertained in princely style.

Still, things did not altogether suit me. Whereat I spoke to Samson Baiersdorf and his wife. «I have no good reason,» I said, «to hasten on my way. But I must insist that my son's wedding take place the first of Nisan. For you know of the betrothals I have concluded for myself, and that I must be in Metz by Lagbeomar. The man has my money already in his hands»[8]—as in truth he had, and, alas, by my own desire.

Samson Baiersdorf told me I might do as I pleased. As for himself, he could not celebrate the marriage before the Feast of Weeks. I should go, if I must, to my own wedding in Metz and take my children with me, and he would give me one hundred ducats to cover my expenses. But this I would not do, nor was it befitting of me.

I resolved to take in patience what I could not change. Although some little differences arose between us with respect to the dowries, they were nicely and honourably settled. And I spent ten weeks in Baiersdorf.

In the month of Sivan the wedding was solemnized with all imaginable pomp. Many eminent persons attended from both sides, and it was celebrated to our general content. May God grant that the young couple enjoy their life in wealth and honour until the Redeemer come, and may their many children grow up to the study of the Torah, and in their days and in ours God send us his Messiah!

6

After the wedding I took my way to Metz, and believed I should pass my old age in peace, and in that pious community work for the good of my soul.

I engaged in Baiersdorf a man named Koppel —he was the *shamash* [beadle]—to accompany me as far as Frankfort, where my husband, so he had written me, had despatched some one to take me the remainder of the journey. So I set forth, first to Bamberg, with my daughter Miriam and the man Koppel.

My son Moses wanted to go with me as far as Bamberg, but I would not permit it, for he was still in the first week of his marriage. We bade each other a fond and sorrowful farewell, and both of us shed many tears. In truth, I was mighty happy to have led my son beneath the wedding canopy and seen that I had, praise God, done well by him —so while my eyes wept, my heart laughed. But such is our nature.

I remained no more than one night in Bamberg. Next morning I took the coach I had ordered long ahead, and made my way to Frankfort.

I could not, however, deter my son Samuel from accompanying me as far as Würzburg. There we said good-bye forever; for the thought lay in both our hearts that we were not to see each other again in this world.

On the 20th of Sivan, 5460 [June 11, 1700], I arrived safe in Frankfort. I was met there by a householder from Metz, named Leser, bearing a letter from my husband. He had sent me *Leb-kuchen* [spice-cake] and other trifles for the journey, and wrote me so courteously I could not dream of the great misfortune lying ahead of me.

I was accorded every honour in Frankfort that a woman could receive, and as indeed I had enjoyed throughout my journey, more in truth than I deserved. Above all I recall the honours paid me in Fürth.

This town of Fürth lies about fifteen miles from Baiersdorf. My son Nathan had sent thither the dowry of my son Moses and the little money I had left—it was little indeed!—in the care of Gabriel Levi. Shall I write of the honours bestowed on me by all his house? I could not, alas, come to an end of them. Not only did the good people put themselves to the pains of procuring me money for my bills of exchange, but they consigned a part of it, on my order, to sundry places; for I put my son's dowry out to interest, until the wedding,

among various persons—Moses Bamberg did me the
favour of taking 1000 thalers, the right learned
Chief Rabbi Mendel Rothschild likewise 1000
thalers, and Loeb Biber of Bamberg another 1000
thalers, and the remainder we loaned out in Baiersdorf.

Afterwards I cast up accounts with Gabriel Levi,
and wanted to pay him, as was proper, his com-
mission. But he refused to take a penny and said
it was no business transaction he had done, but a
plain duty and a good deed. I tried to bring many
convincing reasons to bear. But—no thought of
it!—he had not even deducted the post charges.
May God repay him!

But to return to my journey. Monday I left
Frankfort with my travelling companion Reb
Leser, and also in company with Reb Liebermann
of Halberstadt, whom I had chanced on in Frankfort, as well as the physician Hirz Wallich. And
we enjoyed a pleasant journey together.

Some miles before Metz, my husband's secretary
met us on horse, and rode by our coach until we
came to an inn. He had brought with him all the
food and drink his mount could carry. This secretary, one Lemle Wimpfen, also brought me the
compliments of his master.

After we had eaten and drunk, we drove on for
a matter of two or three hours, and the secretary

Lemle Wimpfen rode by our side. We halted at a
village not five hours from Metz. Before we lay
down to rest, he took leave of us, saying he must
be in Metz betimes.

Although I had been given every impression of
splendour, kindness and wealth, and although my
husband's letters spoke of nothing but respect and
pleasure, nevertheless, God knows, my spirits were
downcast. Whether my heart foresaw the end of
it all or whether it reproached me for taking to
myself another mate, who shall tell? But this way
of thinking were all too late, and with great effort
I forced my heart to silence.

Friday, the 22nd of Sivan, as we approached
within an hour of Metz, we were joined again by
the secretary Lemle Wimpfen, and with him a
companion likewise on horse. They rode beside a
coach, in which sat three distinguished women: the
wife of the Rabbi of Metz, the wife of the Rabbi
Aaron Worms, and the wealthy Frau Jachet,
mother of my son-in-law Moses Krumbach.

They received me with all courtesy and honour.
I needs must sit me in their coach, and so we rode
together into Metz. A great tribute, indeed, for
a mere nobody to be met by three such distinguished ladies—but the tribute was doomed to
sour in my mouth.

When we were hard by Metz we were met by

THE JEWRY OF METZ—LATE SEVENTEENTH CENTURY

Synagogue to Right of Steeple of Church Marked 19—Jewish Cemetery to Right
in Background

a sedan-chair carrying my daughter Esther, who was now near to bearing child.

7

I descended at the house of my son-in-law Moses. He was in Paris at the time, and his mother stayed with my daughter.

The distinguished ladies who had met us on the road now departed with courtly apologies, for it was close to the Sabbath. I thanked them for their trouble as best I could and as my downright German speech had taught me.

Then my daughter prepared me a soup, that I might eat; but my heart was so heavy that I myself despaired to know the reason. I laid it to the wear and tear of travelling.

An hour later, my bridegroom came, together with the rich Abraham Krumbach. They bade me welcome, remained a little, and then went on their way.

At first I did not really know who or which was the bridegroom, for I had never laid eyes on either of them before—until the father of my son-in-law, Abraham Krumbach, said in jest, I should not make the mistake of taking *him* for the groom. And I answered him with silence.[9]

So the time passed, and it was Sabbath. But I did not go to synagogue. My daughter went, for, as everyone can tell you, she never missed a synagogue service. The good name she everywhere enjoyed cannot be described, and it was all the comfort I had, throughout my stay in Metz.

During prayer-time, my stepchildren came and greeted me. I did not recognize them, and no one was present to tell me who they were. So I said to them, «I do not know to whom I am indebted for the honour of this visit, for I am a stranger and have no acquaintance here.» Whereat one of them, Hendele, replied, «Don't you know us? Methinks you are to be our mother.» And I replied, «If I am to be your mother, then you will be my children.» After a few words—since synagogue was over—they departed in all politeness.

When my daughter Esther, together with Isaiah Krumbach, came home from synagogue we sat ourselves to table. As we were eating, in came the lad Abraham, a sort of valet to my husband, together with a maidservant; and they bore two huge gilt trays, one laden with the finest and best sweetmeats, and the other with the finest native as well as imported fruits, such as lemons and Portugal oranges; there were likewise a gold chain with a gold trinket and two large gilden beakers of wine. This was my «Sabbath-fruits» [gift for the Sabbath], and it was rare indeed.

I said to myself, in my heavy mood, «God grant the end will be as good as the beginning.» But, O my Lord and God! the golden chain is turned to iron bonds and fetters.

In another hour, my bridegroom called on me again, together with the rich Frau Jachet, the mother of my son-in-law. They sat with us about thirty minutes, and then they each returned home.

I saw that everything was truly *magnifique* and done with splendour, and I ought to have rejoiced, instead of brooding and brooding over my heavy thoughts. Everyone envied me and told me I must have done a great deal of good in my life to be so lucky as to win a man of his virtues and wealth. Still my heart would not be quiet, and in the end, alas, it proved to be right.

The same Sabbath morning, my daughter Miriam was summoned by my stepdaughter Frommet and likewise given a little gold chain as her «Sabbath-fruits.» So everything passed off nobly.

The letters my son-in-law wrote my daughter from Paris were filled with nothing but *recommendations* for my comfort and entertainment. They showed love and devotion in every line, as they ought. But the love lasted only «until the day broke»[10]—as you shall see. My son-in-law, no doubt, thought he had brought about a good work, and had done well by me.

The week passed without anything else worth remark.

8

Thursday of the following week, the 1st of Tamuz, was my wedding-day. In the morning I was escorted from my daughter's house to a house neighbouring my husband. I sat there till about noon.

The wedding took place at noon, in our summer-garden. Frau Breinle, the wife of the rabbi, and the rich Frau Jachet led me beneath the canopy, and my husband wedded me with a costly ring weighing an ounce in gold.

After the ceremony I was conducted to our chamber off from my husband's cabinet, and it was beautifully furnished. Food was served me, together with the wedding-cake, as is the German custom. Though I had fasted, as I should, the entire day before my wedding, I could not bring myself to touch a bite; for my heart still overflowed with tears. When I had parted from my daughter Esther, we both had wept as only our hearts bade us.

My husband now led me to his cabinet, and showed me a great chest filled with all manner of precious rings and chains. But from that day to this, he did not give me the tiniest ring or so much as a silver coin or medal; and I cannot say he went bankrupt on my account.

A princely dinner was served that evening, with

everything conducted in magnificence. I saw servants and maids everywhere I turned, and wherever I looked or listened, I found nothing but abundance.

His counting-room bulged with silver and gold, and one would never have guessed, from the appearance of things, the outcome of it all. He had long been *parnas* of the community, and truly «at his word they went out and they came in.»[11] Everyone, Jew and Gentile, honoured and obeyed him.

9

During the week following the wedding, the best people came and welcomed and congratulated me. I wished nothing more than to have known French that I might have answered them as I should. But my husband spoke for me.

For a considerable time, everything went along to my heart's content. I wanted for nothing. My husband gave me all the money needed for maintaining the house. I found, however, that the headhousekeeper was «lord and master,» and that everything passed through her hands, all the food, whole sugar-loaves, and other stores, so that she never once asked me what to cook or do.

This hardly pleased me, for in Hamburg I was not used to letting a servant play the lord and master. I spoke about it more than once to my stepchildren and my sister-in-law Freudchen. But they all told me that my predecessor, the departed Blumchen, had always let the head-housekeeper manage everything and placed all in her hands, without a moment's doubt of her faithfulness.

When I entered the house I found two menservants and two maids, besides numerous lackeys. Though I had no liking for it, everyone talked me out of it and said it was nothing compared to the days of his first wife.

To tell the truth, my stepchildren, who were already married, often sighed over the old days and gave me to know all the good and agreeable things their blessed mother was accustomed to bestow on them. I was unable to do the like, and could only send them dainties, which were for all to take, when something special was prepared in the kitchen. When on a Friday I bought them «Sabbath-fruits» for a quarter-thaler or a livre, I was laughed at and told one bought for more than a thaler and sent whole baskets to each and every child.

I allowed all this to pass for a space of time, and thanked God and believed I had brought my long care-ridden widowhood to a happy end, even though it were «joy mixed with trembling.»[12]

My husband was indeed a good man, and as he had represented himself, a rich one. I saw more rare gold and silver than ever had the richest man in Germany. I saw, too, that he conducted a great business, and correctly as well, that no man who had money due him need come asking for it twice, but that he paid everything punctually. He advanced credits everywhere, among Jews and Gentiles, and in every corner of the map. Moreover, he was held to be such a trustworthy and capable man of affairs that everyone who wished to place his money in sure hands brought it to my husband.

Thus, my son-in-law, who left for Paris about a week before my arrival, took all he had and gave it to my husband for safekeeping during his absence. He preferred to leave it with my husband than with his own father. For my husband was considered not only rich, but honourable and reliable, so I little doubted but I had married well.

Of a truth, my husband often groaned in his sleep. I asked him many times what troubled him but he always answered, nothing—it was, he said, his nature and habit to groan in his sleep. I also inquired of his children and my sister-in-law Freudchen, for in the beginning I fancied that living, as everyone said, so happily with his first wife, he was unable as yet to forget her. But they all assured me it was nothing but his custom, and he had groaned of nights when his first wife was still alive. Whereat I thought no more of it, and never suspected the worries hiding beneath his cry in the night.

He slept poorly and ate badly.

10

When I was about eight weeks in Metz, my daughter Esther happily gave birth to her son Elias, which gladdened my heart, for she had lost several lovely children. And we all rejoiced at the darling babe—God be with it!

My husband and I were the god-parents, and as godfather he gave them a costly present, a goblet plated inside and out with above three ounces of gold. When my daughter left her bed, he sent her a doubloon as a «childbed-gift.» She was up and out by the circumcision and oversaw everything. The third day after her son became a Jew, she did the cooking herself for the dinner given in her honour, and everyone marvelled thereat.

Her mother-in-law, the rich Frau Jachet, has often said to me, «I must confess, she is a better cook than I am.» In truth, whenever Frau Jachet wanted something fine prepared, she always called in my daughter Esther; no one else's cooking would do.

I cannot tell you the name my daughter had for piety, breeding, and every virtue, among both high and low. Grieved though she was for the loss of her children, she seldom let it be shown. She was frugal, foresighted and exact in her house-keeping, but it never failed to do her credit. Every day she had a house-rabbi and a Talmud student at her table, and meted out honour and respect to rich and poor alike, so I had reason enough to rejoice in her.

And God took pity on our joy and our incon-stant luck, in the first of my sorrows and griefs at Metz.

On the Day of Atonement my grandchild Elias fell sick, and for eight days lay racked with fits. The child suffered so grievously that more than once I prayed God in my heart to shorten his agony. For neither man nor doctor believed the child could recover. But the Father of goodness, in the flash of an eye, took mercy on him and sent him healing.

Whereat you may learn that God can help when all human effort has failed, and God makes fools of doctors and healers, as it is said, «For I am the Lord that healeth thee.»[13] I praise and thank Him all my days, and may the good and great God grant that his parents lead him to the Torah, the wedding canopy and to deeds of loving kindness![14] It is not hard to imagine my daughter's joy, and how for the new life given to her child she lav-ished large sums on charity—and much of it secretly. For her husband, like so many others, had his heart bound up in mere money.

As it is told of Alexander the Macedon who, as everyone knows, travelled and conquered the whole wide world: Whereat he thought to himself, «I am such a mighty man and I have travelled so far, I must be near to the Garden of Eden.» For he stood by the river Gihon, which is one of the four rivers that flow from the Garden.

So he built himself stout ships, boarded them with all his men, and through his great wisdom reached the fork where you enter towards Eden. When he neared the Garden itself, a fire came and consumed all the ships and men, save Alexander's own ship and its crew.

He now strode to the gate of the Garden and begged to enter, for he wanted to see all the wonders of the world. And a voice answered him and bade him depart, for through this gate «only the righteous may come in.»

After Alexander had pleaded some while in vain, he finally asked that something be tossed him from over the wall, that he might show it as a token to prove that he had at last reached the gate of Eden.

Whereat an eye fell at his feet. He picked it up, without well knowing what to do with it. And a voice told him to heap together all his gold and silver and other goodly possessions and pile them in one scale of a balance, and then lay the eye in the other scale, and the eye would outweigh all the rest.

King Alexander was, it is well known, a great philosopher and a wise man, as his teacher Aristotle had trained him to be, and he sought to master all manner of wisdom. He was loath to believe that a little thing like an eye could outweigh so much heavy gold and silver and other goodly possessions, and he set about to see if it were true.

He brought him a great and mighty pair of balances, and placed the eye in one of its enormous scales. And in the other he poured hundreds and hundreds of gold and silver coins, but the more he poured the higher rose the scale and the eye proved heavier and heavier. And in wonderment he asked the reason.

Then he was told to put the tiniest speck of earth over the eye. He did so, and at once the eye rose as though it weighed a feather, and the scale with the gold and silver came tumbling to the ground.

In greater wonderment than ever, he asked how this came about. And the voice replied:

«Hearken, Alexander! The eye of man, so long as he lives, is never full. The more a man has the more he wants. And therefore the eye outweighs all your silver and gold.

«But once a man dies and a speck of earth is laid over his eye, the eye is satisfied.

«Behold, you may see it, Alexander, in your own life. You were not satisfied with your kingdom and needs must travel and conquer the whole world, till you have come to the place where are the servants and children of God.

«So long, then, as you live you will never be satisfied, and you will always want and take more and more, till you will go and die in a strange land, and not so long now either.

«And once you are placed in the earth, you will be content with six feet of ground, you for whom the whole world was too small.

«Go at once, and speak nor ask no more, for you will not be answered.»

So Alexander sailed with his ship to the land of Hodu, where he presently met a terrible and bitter death. For he died of poisoning, as his teacher Aristotle tells us in his history.

A penny honestly earned is hard to part with. But man must learn to control his greed. For 'tis a universal proverb, «Stinginess never enriches and measured generosity never makes one poor.» To everything there is a time—a time to get money and a time to give. And the Dutch say, *Gelt autzugeben in siner tid, dat makt profit*. There are many Gentile sages who have written very wondrously of these things.

11

The illness of my grandchild was the first storm that broke on me in Metz. And, God pity me, it did not end with that.

It happened to me as to the man who fled before the Angel of Death and sought to find refuge in the city of Lus, where no man dies.[15] As he reached the city gate, the Angel of Death said to him, «You did well to come to this gate, for I was given power over you nowhere else in the world but here.»

I, too, fled from Hamburg, from my home, my children, and all my friends, and I thought to myself, «I will go so far from them, that I shall see no evil befall either them or myself.» But Thou, O righteous God, hast shown me and showeth me still, I cannot flee from Thy wrath. «Whither shall I flee from thy presence?»[16]

I find I have come to a place where I have few friends and little peace, but where I see and hear sorrow and vexation heaped upon my beloved children and myself. In all this, I do acknowledge God to be a righteous Judge, for He has given me patience to learn that my distress is common enough the lot of man, and my punishment—as the physician said in my first book—might well have been worse.

It was not long before I received the sorrowful

tidings that my son Loeb was dead—before his twenty-eighth year.

For all the vexations and griefs he had brought me, his death was still a heavy and bitter blow, as it would be to any parent. The good King David, we read, suffered much wrong and grief from his son Absalom; but when he waged war against Absalom he ordered his men to spare his life, and when he learned of his death, he wept bitterly and he cried seven times, «Oh, my son Absalom, my son!» And thereafter he delivered him from the seven circles of hell, and brought him to the Garden of Eden.

So I pardon from the bottom of my heart all that my son did in the years of his youth. He allowed himself, alas, to be led astray, for apart from that he was the best man in all the world, he studied beautifully, and he had a Jewish heart for all the poor and needy, so that the name of his good deeds spread far and wide. Unluckily, he was altogether too careless in business, and wicked men took note of it and despoiled him of his all. But I will now let him rest in peace, and I pray God he may enjoy the merits of those who have gone before him. What should or can I do? «I shall go to him, but he shall not return to me.»[17]

It had not pleased Almighty God to take me before my good and pious husband Chayim Hameln, who could have still been among the living. But «the righteous is taken away from the evil to come.»[18] He died in riches and saw naught but good of his children. But what more can I say of this?—I have spoken of it enough.

And so I will close my sixth book. May the Almighty God spare us and all Israel from further evil, and in His great mercy and grace forgive us sinners all our debts, and lead us back to the Holy Land, that our eyes may see the rebuilding of Thy holy house and our glory restored!

Forgive us our sins, as it is written «Then will I sprinkle clean water upon you, and ye shall be clean.»[19]

THE END OF MY SIXTH BOOK

BOOK SEVEN

1

WITH God's help I will begin my seventh book, which contains both pleasures and pains, as does the world itself. God grant I suffer no more sorrow in my children, and that in my old age I see and hear naught but good of them.

As I told you, I bade good-bye forever to my son Samuel. God have mercy on us, that so young and brave a man must bite the black of earth!

I was not two years here in Metz when the doleful tidings came. Not long after his death, his wife gave birth to a daughter—praise God, a sound and healthy child. She is now about thirteen years of age and must be a fine grown-up girl. She lives with her grandfather in Bamberg.

Her mother took to herself another husband, but did not keep him for long, as, alas, he died. And the good young woman has spent her best years to this day in sorrow. «But who will say, What doest thou?»[1] I can speak no more of it, for my heart's grief.

2

At the end of my first year here, I thought I should live out my life in peace, as I had every reason to believe. And if my husband could have held out two years longer, he would have well cleared himself of his difficulties. For two years after he surrendered all he had to his creditors, business flourished so mightily in France that all Metz became rich.

My husband was exceedingly able, and a great business man, and highly esteemed by Jew and Gentile. But the God of goodness had willed otherwise, and his creditors pressed him so sorely that he crashed on the rocks and all was lost.

Though his creditors received but half of what was due them, they treated him with great clemency. Even I renounced my claims on certain sums due me from the wedding, for I saw myself there was nothing to be gotten.

He had all the money of my daughter Miriam in his hands, but I managed to get it back in the form of bills on other Jews. But God knows the bitterness of it. My son Nathan had claims on him as well, to the amount of several thousands, and I brought it about that he too was paid.

In all this I gave no thought to my own wedding-portion, but took with what grace I could all that God allotted me, like the eagle that hid its

fledglings beneath its wings and said, better they
shoot me than my little ones.

Yet how I suffered! My husband was forced to
take himself into hiding. When his creditors discovered he was gone, they despatched three bailiffs to our house. They made an inventory of everything, to the nails on the walls, and wrote it
down and sealed everything up, so I had not food
enough by me for a meal.

I lived together with my housekeeper in one
room. The three bailiffs made themselves master
of this as well, and no one could enter or leave.
Once when I sought to leave, they put me to search,
lest I hid something on me.

Three weeks we lived in this miserable state.
Finally, my husband reached an accord with his
creditors. They wrote down everything he had,
and then left it all in his hands, that he call an
auction. Not a pewter spoon escaped writing down,
so that nothing could be concealed.

Nor did my husband wish to conceal anything,
For he thanked God he could escape with his life.
His creditors saw that he had in truth rendered
all he owned, so they took pity on him, even though
he could not pay the half he had agreed upon.
They let him go in peace, though they could well
have thrust him into prison. But they knew him
for an honest man and saw that neither skin nor
bone remained to him.

He was indeed a good and honourable man, and in his prosperous days he was esteemed and loved by everyone. For thirty years he was *parnas* and *schtadlan*[2] of Metz, and his behaviour in these offices won him the love of Jew and Gentile.

After he had come to grief, we lived in the direst misery, and time and again there was no bread in the house. Since, at that period, living became very dear in Metz, I was forced to lay out money from my own little hoard to buy the barest needs. But as quickly as my husband came by a few livres he always repaid me.

3

My son-in-law Moses Krumbach helped my husband generously, though he had lost over 2000 thalers in the crash. The great and good God favoured my son-in-law so that, praise God, he became the richest man in the community, and righteous withal.

He was given a new heart, so that he lavished much good on his kin, both on his side and on the side of my daughter Esther.

Today he is *parnas*, his house stands open to the poor, and all distinguished visitors, who come, indeed, from the four corners of the earth, enjoy his hospitality; and he shows them due respect and courtesy, quite like his dear wife Esther. Both of them are blessed with great hearts, and much good comes from their house. God reward him, and keep him and his children in honours, riches, and the best of health for a hundred years and more!

It was about the year 5472 [1712] on the 1st of Sivan, when my grandchild Elias—Esther's son —became a bridegroom, blessings and happiness upon him! The wedding was set for four years later, for both bride and groom were exceedingly young—God lengthen their days and years. Together their dowries only amounted to 30,000 Reichsthalers!

4

My husband had few to help him in his distress. His children were in no position to bring him what he needed, though they did what they could.

Rabbi Samuel Lévy, the son of my luckless husband, was a mighty Talmud scholar, and in every way an energetic and capable man. He had long been in Poland, where he had so perfected his studies he won the title of *Morenu* [Our Master]. He had returned to Metz some years before my arrival, and I found him established there in his own house.

Both my husband and Rabbi Samuel's father-in-law, the rich and pious Abraham Krumbach, had so provided for him that he could continue his learned pursuits. Through their authority they helped him to receive a rabbinate, I believe, in

Alsace; and he exercised his office with great wisdom. Moreover he was well beloved of all men.

«But a handful does not satisfy a lion.» The returns from a rabbinate could not meet the needs of his household. For both Rabbi Samuel and his wife Genendel came from princely houses, kept up in a grand style and dispensing bounties on all sides. So Rabbi Samuel engaged himself in the service of the Duke of Lorraine.

At that time His Highness held his court in Lunéville, because of the war raging between the King of France and the Kaiser together with his allies, whom I need not name, for everyone knows who they were.[3]

Rabbi Samuel engaged himself to take over the mint for the aforesaid Duke. But he needed for this purpose a larger capital than he could furnish alone.

Six months previously he had likewise opened shop in Lunéville, and for this, too, large capital was needed, inasmuch as His Highness and all his court bought their entire supplies from him—so high he stood in the favour of the Duke and his Counsellors, as well he might, for he was one of those who found favour in the sight of God and men.

When he saw he could not handle his store alone, he took both of his brothers-in-law from Metz into the business. One of them, Isai Willstadt, who

was married to Rabbi Samuel's sister, was a promi-
nent member of the community; and the other,
Jacob Krumbach, the brother of my son-in-law
Moses, was likewise a big and substantial man.

All three left behind them their fine houses in
the *Judengasse* [Jewry] of Metz and moved to
Lunéville. They created a partnership, and stocked
their store with wares which sold readily. They
likewise engaged in other trade, so they found
themselves nicely placed. Thereafter, Rabbi Samuel undertook the mintage, on which it is true
he could not earn overmuch. But the run of folks
imagined all sorts of beautiful profits.

He wrote of the undertaking to his father, but
my husband greatly disapproved of it. My husband
had an excellent head for business and knew that
such an enterprise could come to no good, above
all since it would hardly please the King of France.
For our city lies hard by Lunéville, only a day's
journey away, and the money that was coined
would all flow to Metz.

My husband weighed the whole matter, as the
shrewd and practised man of business that he was,
and wrote his son in detail of the great amount of
capital required and the small profits to be enjoyed.
But the three partners were young and warmly
won to the affair, and they concluded a contract
with His Highness the Duke to deliver him large

quantities of silver, and take a share of the coinage in payment for minting it.

For a while all went merrily; but a quantity of the coins were poorly struck, and the downfall of Rabbi Samuel came about as you will hear.[4]

5

For six months the partners conducted their store, and dealt in money and bills and the like, as is the custom of the Jews.

At that time, one Moses Rothschild lived in Metz. He was a man of great means, for many years he had traded in Lorraine, and he was well known among the merchants. When he heard of the thriving business of our three partners, he, too, removed to Lunéville, together with his son who had married Rabbi Samuel's daughter. Through the influence of the Duke's advisers, for he stood high in their eyes, Moses Rothschild settled close to the city and likewise engaged himself to deliver silver to the mint.

Their common business prospered, and Rabbi Samuel helped his father in many ways, so my husband never fell into want.

The partners sent on money to Metz; sometimes it was seized and returned to them, but other times, when it was seized, that was the last they heard of it. Meanwhile my husband worried greatly, for he saw the many risks and dangers of the business, and more than once wrote his son of his fears. But it proved useless; there was no changing what was done.

Meanwhile, the war between the King of France and the Kaiser grew in bitterness, and finally the King of France forbade the import or export of Lorraine money.

Furthermore, the King's minister delivered a royal letter to M. Latandy[5] of Metz, to be sent in turn to the Jewish community for public reading. The letter mentioned by name the five Jews who had formerly lived in our city and who were now doing business in Lorraine. They were told that if they remained in Lorraine, they would be forbidden, under severe penalty, to set foot in France as long as they lived. They were given a certain number of months to make their choice: Lunéville and Lorraine, or Metz and France.[6]

When our five men heard the tidings they were badly frightened, and they knew not what to decide. Each had left behind him a valuable house. Moreover, they did not fancy having to surrender their right of residence in Metz. And added thereto, they had engaged themselves, under heavy fine, to carry on the mintage for the Duke of Lorraine.

At last the time for decision arrived. Isai Willstadt decided first—and elected to return to Metz. Then Jacob Krumbach did likewise. I do not know how they managed to release themselves from the

Duke; but what they owned in goods they divided between them, and returned here with their wives and children, and took up their former abodes.

But Rabbi Samuel and Moses Rothschild, together with his son, resolved to stay in Lorraine.

6

My husband fell ill at the tidings, and he took them so to heart that he succumbed beneath the worry and anguish of it. For he was ever a sickly man and had suffered woefully from the gout, and now this added blow struck him to the ground.

His son Rabbi Samuel saw that he lacked for nothing, sending him whatever he needed, and ordered his agent in Metz to provide him with whatever he asked for, but all his care proved of no avail. Rabbi Samuel sent him a highly reputed physician to apply various cures. The physician remained at his side a number of days and tried his remedies; but as soon as he had laid eyes on him, he said, the man is doomed—as the event proved.

The Almighty God took him back to Himself forever, and of a surety he dwells in the world to come.

He was *parnas* of the community for long years, and he had in truth risked his life in its defence—of which much could be written. But I do not find it necessary.

He went to eternal peace, and left me sitting with my cares and woes.[7]

7

I received back very little of the money from my wedding-contract, not a third of what was due me.

And then? I left myself in the hands of the All-bountiful God.

I was living at the time in the house of Isai Willstadt, which had once belonged to my husband, and I had thought to remain there to the end of my days, as indeed Reb Isai had assured me I could. But when my husband died and Isai Willstadt returned to Metz with his wife and children and his furniture as well, I was compelled to leave the house.[8]

And I knew not where to go. I could not stay with my son-in-law Moses Krumbach, for his house was not yet built, as now, praise God, it is. So I was very badly off.

Finally, one Jacob Marburg allowed me to build a tiny room in his house. I had neither hearth nor chimney. I had to cook in his kitchen and spend the winter days by his fireside. But when time came to sleep, or for any reason I must go to my room, I had to climb a flight of twenty-two steps. It was so hard for me that usually I abandoned the effort.

Once when I was sick—it was in Tebet, 5475 [January, 1715]—my son-in-law Moses visited me and said to me, I must dwell with him. He wanted to give me a room on the ground floor of his house, to save me climbing stairs. But I refused his offer, as I had many reasons for wishing never to live with my children.

However, as things went, I could hold out no longer. Life grew very dear that year in Metz, and I had to keep some one to take care of me. I was also putting the community to expense in helping me, so I finally yielded to what I had so long refused, and moved into the home of my son-in-law Moses Krumbach.

This was in 5475 [1715], and I am writing these lines in Tamuz of the same year. My son-in-law and my daughter—long may they live!—and their children—God be with them!—were well contented with me.

Shall I write you of how they treated me? There would be too much to tell. May the Father of goodness reward them! They paid me all the honours in the world. The best of everything was placed on my plate, more than I wanted or deserved, and I fear lest God count these bounties against my merits, which, alas, are few enough.

If I were not at table when they dined—for they ate at the stroke of noon—and at this hour psalms were read in synagogue for the soul of his pious mother, the blessed Frau Jachet—they have been read these many years and doubtless will continue to be read until the Messiah comes—when I would return home from synagogue, I always found my dinner awaiting me, three or four of the most tasty dishes, far beyond my wants. I often used to say to my daughter, «At least leave me room to breathe!» But she would answer me, «I cook neither more nor less because of you.» And it was the truth.

I have visited many communities in my life, but never have I seen such hospitality as hers. One and all were received with welcome and respect at her table, charity guests as well as invited guests. The blessed Lord of all bounties keep them for a hundred years in health and peace, and in riches and honour!

8

Were I to write of what else happened, or if the Jews here lived up to their name for piety, I could only say that when I first came here, Metz was a very beautiful and pious community, and the *parnassim* were all worthy men who verily adorned the council-room.

In those days not a man who sat in the council-room wore a *perruque*, and no one heard of a man

going out of the *Judengasse* [Jewry] to bring a
case before a Gentile tribunal. When differences
arose, and there were many, as there always are
among Jews, they were one and all settled before
the communal or rabbinical courts. No such ar-
rogance reigned in the old days as now, and people
were not wont to eat such costly meals. The children applied themselves to learning, and the elders
time and again had the ablest known rabbis serve
the community.

In my days the right learned Rabbi Gabriel
Eskeles was rabbi, and head of the Talmud school.
His great piety needs no mention, for it is known
the world over, and it is not for me to dwell upon
his excellencies, for I could not describe the half,
nay, the tenth of them.

His son married the daughter of the rich and
mighty Samson Wertheimer of Vienna; the dowries, together with the wedding-gifts, amounted
to more than 30,000 Reichsthalers. Rabbi Gabriel
took his wife, his son Loeb, and the bridegroom
Rabbi Berich, to Vienna; and the wedding was
celebrated with a pomp hitherto unknown among
the Jews.

But why write at length of such matters, when I
cannot give you all the details? It is better to pass
them off with a word, for they are well enough
known without me.

9

The pious and most profoundly learned Rabbi Gabriel—may his light shine!—received a year's leave of absence from the community, but they never thought that he would stay out his leave. However, the one year lengthened into nearly three.

When the third year drew to its close, the *parnassim* wrote him, with all the reverence in the world, that he might still return to his place in peace; for the community was like a shepherdless flock, and such a community cannot well endure without a worthy rabbi. I might say, however, there were in truth able men, great Talmud scholars and sages enough in Metz; above all that Prince of the Law, the venerable Rabbi Aaron Worms, many years rabbi of Mannheim and thereabouts, as well as rabbi in Alsace.

This Rabbi Aaron had married his son to the grand-daughter of Rabbi Gabriel. Accordingly, Rabbi Aaron belonged to Rabbi Gabriel's party in Metz, and maintained he would surely return. Since Rabbi Aaron was an exceedingly wise man, deeply versed in both religious and wordly matters, his word carried great weight. And the community contented itself to wait a while longer.

Finally, word came to the ears of the community that Rabbi Gabriel had been named for rabbi of Nikolsburg.[9] I cannot begin to tell of the strife that now arose.

The son of Rabbi Gabriel appeared in Metz and sought to persuade the communal authorities to continue waiting. But after they heard that Rabbi Gabriel had allowed himself to be named for rabbi in Nikolsburg, the authorities decided, with the approval of the greater part of the community, to betake to themselves another rabbi. Thereat the storm broke.

The partisans of Rabbi Gabriel, such as Rabbi Aaron and his men, did all in their power to prevent the naming of another rabbi. But, presently, at a great meeting of all the community, the authorities bound themselves, under penalty of a heavy fine, to choose a successor.

Whereat they wrote a call-letter, worded with due respect, to Chief Rabbi Broda of Prague, and despatched it with a special courier. After some time, and after certain changes in the contract were conceded by the authorities, the aforementioned rabbi agreed to come.

Whether the highly venerable Rabbi Gabriel heard of this offer, or whether he had always meant to come back to his post, I cannot say; but in any case, he now returned and proposed, with the support of his partisans, to reoccupy his rabbinate.

I dare not write of all that happened. God forgive each and every one of us for our sins! Far be it from a humble simple woman like myself to write of such things. God forgive everyone for what he did in party heat!—but I could fill a whole book of what they did, both parties of them, to win their will. As for my part, I pray God give us to enjoy the virtue and piety of both these sages in Israel.

After Rabbi Gabriel had remained here for a space, and seen there was nothing to be done, and that the authorities could not withdraw their written offer after Rabbi Abraham Broda had said that he would come, he again departed—and with all honours; for the whole community was his friend.

10

I will curb my pen, and merely say that Rabbi Abraham Broda arrived in due time. I need not describe the honour he commanded in Metz, it is too well known. They built him no less than a house of his own, with his own schoolroom and his own master's chair, and I am fain to believe, as far as my poor knowledge goes, the like has never been done before.

Of his person,[10] his erudition and his good works, there is much to say, above all, of the learning he brought to the community and how he gave day and night to his studies and to carrying the Torah to Israel. He took children who truly knew little or nothing and made of them diligent students. His knowledge of Torah was famed the length and breadth of the land.

But our joy was soon at an end. The great scholar allowed himself to be elected rabbi of Frankfort. For all that our authorities pressed him to remain and offered him whatever his heart desired, he stood by his decision.

Since his departure, we have had naught but bad times—much sickness and great losses of money. Many vigorous young women have died—of whom, otherwise, nothing evil was known. Misery has prevailed. May God look upon us again in mercy, and remove His wrath from us and from all Israel!

11

I cannot refrain from telling of the disaster that befell our community on the Sabbath of the Feast of Weeks in the year 5475 [May, 1715].

Men, women and children were all in the synagogue. The great singer, Cantor Jokel of Rzeszow in Poland, had begun to chant the morning prayers. He was singing on from the passage «Thou art God in Thy power and might» and his sweet voice had not reached the words «Blessed art Thou who formest light» when many present heard a noise as though something were breaking overhead.

The womenfolk in the upper balcony thought the ceiling was about to fall, and because of the great rumbling noise like stones grinding loose, a mighty fear came upon them and they scrambled to leave the building. Each one thought of nothing but to save her own life.

They poured in a rush down the stairs, and those that fell were trodden beneath the heels of the others. In less than a few minutes six women perished and more than thirty were wounded, some of them nigh unto death, so that they lay for months in the hands of chirurgeons.

If they had made their escape in good order, no one would have been hurt. Among them was an old blind woman; she could not run and needs must remain in her seat «till the wrath be overpast.»[11] Whereat nothing happened to her, and she reached home as she had left it.

The survivors came running out into the street, for the most part, alas, with hair uncovered[12] and with their clothing nigh torn from their bodies.

A few of them told me afterwards that they wanted to escape but found no means, so they had returned to their places and said, «If we must die, better in the synagogue than squeezed to death on the stairs!» For more than fifty women lay knitted and writhing together on the steps, glued to one another as with pitch, living and dead in one mass.

The menfolk came running to them, each one bent on rescuing his own. But only with difficulty could the women be wrenched and pried apart.

THE FEAST OF WEEKS IN A SOUTH GERMAN SYNAGOGUE

Upper and Lower Balconies for the Women to be Seen at Right

Many burghers came hurrying to the *Judengasse*, bearing ladders and axes, not knowing what had befallen.

The men in the synagogue had likewise heard the rumbling noise, and believed as well that the roof was falling in, and they began screaming to their womenfolk, begging them to flee, and so heightened the terror and disorder.

You can imagine the desolation everywhere—six women dead, six young women who a moment before were in the fullness of their vigour and health. God have mercy on us, and withdraw His wrath from us and from all Israel!

12

The womenfolk who were seated in the lower gallery were also badly alarmed and pressed one upon the other.

Your mother, children dear, was in her seat in the lower gallery, absorbed in the prayers. I heard the noise of the women running above me, and I asked a neighbour what it could mean. My neighbour thought it was a woman with child who had fallen ill. Whereat I took fright, for my daughter Esther, sitting about six places from me, was likewise expectant.

I hastened to her in the great press, as she was making to crowd her way out, and I cried to her,

«Where are you going?» She answered, «The roof is tumbling down!»

Whereat I lay hold of her, and with my own hands forced our way towards the door.

When you leave the lower gallery, you must descend five or six steps. As I fought my way out with my daughter, I fell on the lowest step, and knew no more. And none came to my aid.

The men hastening to the rescue of their women-folk passed the place where I lay without life or motion, and had it lasted a moment longer, I would have been trampled to my death.

But finally the men saw me, and helped me up, so that I reached the street. Whereupon I began to scream and ask what had happened to my daughter. And they told me she had gone home.

At once I sent some one off to see if she were there. The answer came that she had not returned. And I began running about as though I had lost my mind.

My daughter Miriam saw me, and joyful at the sight of me, came running to my side. I asked her, «Where is my Esther?» And she told me—in the house of my brother-in-law Reuben.

I ran to his house, which is not far from the synagogue, and there I found my daughter sitting in a faint, without veil or mantle. Men and women stood about trying to revive her. And, thank God, she recovered, with no harm to her unborn babe.

The greater part of the victims were likewise with child; but they went to their rest, and to us remained the pain and woe. On the day after the Feast of Weeks, the burial-brotherhood went to the graveyard in the early of the morning, and the six women were placed side by side beneath the black earth.

13

Later, the women's section of the building was carefully gone over, but nothing was found amiss. And to this day we do not know the reason for the terrible rumbling noise.

We must presume it was sent for our sins. Woe unto us that we had lived to see this thing, and the word of God fulfilled, «I will send a faintness into their hearts in the lands of their enemies; and the sound of a shaken leaf shall chase them; and they shall fall when none pursueth.»[13] That it should happen on this holy Sabbath day, the day our Holy Torah was given us, the day that God had chosen us from among all peoples and tongues![14] Truly we were «become a reproach to our neighbours, a scorn and derision to them that are round about us.»[15] It was as though in our own days the Holy Temple were destroyed.

Many were the stories told of the disaster, but who can write or believe all one hears? Frau Esther, the wife of our present teacher, Reb Jacob, was sitting with her five-year-old child at the top of the steps. Suddenly she saw six very tall women with little flowing veils hurrying over her down the stairs. She cried out, «Do you want to kill me and my child?» Whereupon they took the child and placed it in a corner where it was spared all harm. And then they went on their way. It was not till that moment came the terrible noise, and the terror began. This Frau Esther was always an upright woman and never known to tell a lie.

Again, in the night before the disaster, the wife of the rich Jacob Krumbach, whose house stands next to the synagogue, heard a great noise in it, as though thieves were tearing everything to pieces and the lights were crashing down. The woman awakened her husband, and they sent for the *shamas* [beadle] who unlocked the synagogue, but naught was found, not even a morsel of plaster fallen from its place.

And so it is unknown «for whose cause this evil is upon us.»[16]

For myself, I cannot but think it hearkens back to the sins committed on the previous feast of Simhat Torah [Rejoicing of the Law]. As customary on that occasion, all the holy Scrolls of the Law were taken from the holy Ark, and seven of them stood on a table.

At that moment a brawl broke out among the womenfolk, and they tore one from another the

veils from their heads, so that they stood uncovered in the synagogue. Whereat the men joined in
the fray, and set upon one another with blows.
Although the learned Rabbi Abraham bade them
at the top of his voice and under threat of the ban,
cease in God's name defiling the holy day, it served
to no purpose.

Thereafter, the rabbi and the *parnassim* left the
synagogue; and in due time they decreed the proper
punishment for each offender.

14

In the month of Nisan, 5479 [1719], a woman
was kneeling by the bank of the Moselle, washing
her dishes. It was about ten o'clock at night, and
of a sudden it became as light as day, and the
woman looked in the Heavens, and the Heavens
were opened, like unto a . . . [word illegible]
. . . and sparks flew therefrom; and then the
Heavens closed, as one closes a curtain, and all was
dark again. God grant that it be for our good!

THE END

Notes

All Biblical quotations in the present translation are taken directly or indirectly from the Authorized Version.

Introduction

[1] A by no means exhaustive list of the French and Latin words used by Glückel and typical of the German of her century includes the following: assistiren (assister —*to aid*), Aestimation, Akkord, Accident, accompagniren, accomodiren, blessiren (blesser), Copulation (*wedding*), Collation, consumiren (consummer), Correspondent, canaille, continuiren (continuer), changiren (changer—*as in Fr. not with respect to money*), Confitur, contraren, Differenzen, divertiren (*to amuse*), sich engagiren (s'engager), Effekt, in genere (*Latin*), Historie (histoire—*a happening*), magnifique, miserable, observiren, Provision, Pulcell (pucelle—*maidservant*), passiren (passer—passer le temps), preien

(prier—*ask*), resolviren, Respekt, remir-
tiren, ruiniren (ruiner), Resolution, in
summa (*Latin*).

Book One

[1] Rabbi Akiba said, «Thou shalt love thy neighbour as thyself—that is the greatest commandment.» Sifra, *Kadoshim*, IV, 12.

[2] Talmudic gloss on Ecc. 5: 1.

[3] Shammai said, «Set a fixed time for thy study of the Torah.» *Sayings of the Fathers*, I, 15.

[4] Rabbah said, «When one stands at the judgment-seat of God, these questions are asked: Hast thou been honest in all thy dealings? Hast thou set aside a portion of thy time for the study of Torah? Hast thou observed the First Commandment? Hast thou, in trouble, still hoped and believed in God? Hast thou spoken wisely?» Talmud, *Shabbat*, 31-a.

[5] For a long time two schools disputed about the value of life, one asserting the superiority of existence and the other of non-existence. Finally both schools agreed: «Non-existence is better than existence, but since man has been created, let him apply himself to good works.» Talmud, *Erubin*, 13-b.

[6] *Kohelet Rabbah*, I, 34.

[7] Charles X of Sweden overran Denmark in 1657-58.

[8] *Nebbich* is a common Judeo-German expression of pity; it may be rendered as «alas» or «poor thing!»

[9] *Sephardim* (sing. *Sephardi*; adj. *Sephardic*) are Spanish-Portuguese Jews; they were settled in Hamburg by the last quarter of the sixteenth century and hence long before the German Jews. Unlike the latter, they possessed communal recognition and individual rights. They were engaged in international trade and banking, and members of their community officially represented the business interests of the Portuguese, Swedish and Polish courts.

[10] That is to say, the governmental taxes were not collected from the individual Jews by the heads of the Jewish community.

[11] Is. 26:20. I have substituted the word «wrath» for «indignation.»

[12] In 1648 the Cossacks, under the leadership of Chmielnicki, revolted against the Poles; they ravaged eastern Poland and wrought terrible destruction of life and property among the Jewish communities.

[13] Rabbi Jochanan used to say, «Well for him who has won a good name and with a good name has passed out of the world. Of him Solomon hath said (Ecc. 7:1), A good

name is better than precious ointment and the day of death than the day of one's birth.» Talmud, *Berakot*, 17-a.

[14] I Kings 2:2.

Book Two

[1] It was the custom of well-to-do German Jews to send their children of promise to Poland, which was famous for its schools of Talmudic learning.

[2] A feast held on the Friday before a wedding.

[3] Leffmann Behrens (Liepmann Cohen) was financial agent and purveyor to the dukes of Hanover. His influence made him a powerful patron and intercessor in behalf of the Jews of Brunswick-Lüneburg. Naturally he was *parnas* of the Hanoverian Jewish community. Born about 1630; died, Hanover, 1714.

[4] Allusion to I Sam. 2:7.

[5] Ps. 49:10.

[6] «It can be proved by the Law, the Prophets and the Writings that a man is led along the road he wishes to follow.» Talmud, *Maccoth*, 10-b.

[7] Allusion to Gen. 12:1.

[8] Glückel wrote the first five of her «books» while she was still in Hamburg.

Book Three

[1] Glückel was only 17 when this book

opens; she was nearly 25 at the period with which it closes.

[2] About two miles.

[3] Judah Berlin (Jost Liebmann—died, 1701) became the financial agent and court jeweller of the Great Elector, and later of his son, Elector Frederick III and King Frederick I of Prussia. As court Jew, he succeeded Israel Aaron, whose widow he married. He wielded great influence at the court of Berlin, and enjoyed many privileges, including the right to his own synagogue, and not least, the exemption from paying the head-tax laid only upon Jews. One of his posterity was Meyerbeer the composer.

[4] Lam. 5:16.

[5] Adapted from Is. 26:18.

[6] Repentance, prayer and charity are the three traditional means for procuring forgiveness of sin. They are likewise practised in the face of danger or disaster, to avert an evil visited upon man for his sins.

[7] Sabbatai Zevi (born, 1626), the foremost Messianic pretender in modern Jewish history, heralded his claims from the East. He set the whole Jewish world astir and furnished much speculation among the Christians. Even Oldenburg, the secretary of the Royal Society in London, dropped his philosophic and scientific puzzles to

address an inquiry on the subject to Spinoza.

[8] Ex. 15:20.

[9] The last day of the Feast of Booths, or Harvest Festival, and the most festive celebration of the year in ancient Jerusalem. Contemporaries liked to say of it, Whoever has not seen the Feast of the Water-Drawing has never seen a real festival.

[10] The women sit apart from the men in a synagogue conducted according to tradition and law.

[11] Such would be the decision according to Jewish law.

[12] A traditional manner of prayer in times of great distress.

[13] Talmud, *Berakot*, 33-b.

[14] Hamburg *banko* was currency worth one-half of one per cent more than the ordinary species of the Reich.

[15] Gen. 14:21.

[16] Jews had not been allowed to live in Saxony since 1537. Their presence at the Leipzig Fair was tolerated because of the high tax they were compelled to pay. The forfeiture of goods upon death was not an uncommon measure, nor were Jews always its victims. We may remember Laurence Sterne's fears lest he die in France and forfeit his half-dozen shirts and black silk breeches.

[17] Talmud, *Berakot*, 3-b. The original reads «a handful.»

[18] Jewish legal procedure in such circumstances demands that each party to the dispute appoint a «judge» and these in turn select a third «judge,» whereupon all three «judges» hear the case and render the verdict.

[19] Ecc. 6:10.

[20] I Sam. 16:7.

[21] Talmud, *Shabbat*, 119-a.

[22] Glückel repeats this promise but never fulfils it.

[23] Technically, a *responsum*, or opinion based on Jewish law.

[24] Talmud, *Berakot*, Mishna IX, 3.

[25] *Beroshit Rabbah*, 68.

[26] Probably the French war (under Louis XIV) against Holland, 1672-78.

[27] Num. 27:17.

[28] Glückel means that the communal leaders thought that refusal to pay would have brought discredit on the Jewish community, and hence would have been a «profanation of the name of God.» A similar thought underlies her remark, in the first episode of Book Four, when she says that the thief who preferred to die rather than embrace Christianity «sanctified the name of God.»

[29] Prov. 21:1.

[30] Talmud, *Berakot*, Mishna IX, 5.
[31] A great rabbi and hero in Talmudic days, Jochanan ben Zakkai belonged to the school of Hillel, lived through the fall of Jerusalem, and died in Jabneh about 108 C.E.

Book Four

[1] Elias or Elijah Cleve (Elijah Gomperz—died, 1675) belonged to a prominent Jewish family. He founded a large banking house in Emmerich, and later a bank and store in Berlin. He was a close business adviser of the Great Elector, a banker for the Dutch government and purveyor to the Dutch armies. He was, as we should say today, the «representative» Jew of Cleves. His son Kossmann, who married Glückel's daughter Zipporah, was a printer and publisher in Amsterdam. Kossmann's grandson was the teacher of Moses Mendelssohn.

[2] The Great Elector was an ally of the Dutch in their defence against the predatory campaigns of Louis XIV. Cleves lay in an exposed position.

[3] Talmud, *Sota*, 2-a.

[4] Prince Frederick became, through the death of his older brother (1674), Prince Elector, later Elector of Brandenburg, and finally (1701) the first king of Prussia.

[5] Schechter (*Studies in Judaism*, second series, p. 137), in his admirable essay on Glückel, quotes a reference to the Dance of Death describing it as a «merry sport in which kissing is not forgotten.»

[6] Gen. 13:3. Glückel does not quote the verse in full, but alludes rather to its traditional interpretation which assumes that Abraham step by step retraced his journey.

[7] Hanover was likewise engaged with the Dutch in the war against France.

[8] Schools of higher learning were as reactionary in Glückel's time as they are in Germany and Eastern Europe today.

[9] Samuel Oppenheimer of Heidelberg (1635?-1703) was the first Jew allowed to settle in Vienna after the expulsion of 1670. He became the chief purveyor of the Austrian armies on both the French and Turkish fronts. He thereupon used his profits to become the court banker to Leopold I. When he died the Austrian monarchy owed him millions which were naturally never repaid. His influence, like that of all court Jews, was enormous.

[10] The name of God.

[11] At that time and until 1720 Pomerania belonged to Sweden.

[12] Rabbi Model Ries, originally of Vienna, was the first to be buried in the Jewish cemetery of Berlin. It should be noted, in

connection with the alliance struck between his family and the Hamelns, that
matchmaking was a common procedure at
German and Polish fairs.

[13] Louis XIV's third war of conquest against
the Dutch and their allies. Bonn fell into
the hands of the French in 1688.

[14] Talmud, *Berakot,* 54-b.

[15] Gen. 48:1.

[16] Gen. 37:3.

[17] Mourners for parents recite the *kaddish,* or
sanctification of God, at every synagogal
service for one year after their loss. At least
ten men are required to render a religious
service valid, hence the number of Talmud
scholars engaged by Chayim Hameln, both
for at home and on his journey.

[18] Customary expression used in describing
the death of a righteous man.

[19] Abraham Krumbach's wife was Elias
Cleve's daughter, hence the «kinship» with
Glückel.

[20] Tamid, I, 2.

[21] Household feast on the first Friday evening
after the birth of a son.

[22] Benedictions over wine, light and spices
«separating» the close of the Sabbath from
the workaday week to come.

[23] A Christian woman hired to do the necessary household work forbidden to Jews on
the Sabbath.

²⁴ Adapted from Ps. 128:3.
²⁵ Lam. 3:23.

Book Five

¹ At monthly periods and after childbirth
Jewish women are, according to the Law,
ritually «unclean.» They are «cleansed» by
bathing according to the prescribed fashion
in a specially arranged bath—before which
they are forbidden to the touch of a man.
² The *Shné Luchot Ha-Brit* (*The Two
Tables of the Covenant*), a pious work by
the Frankfort rabbi, Isaiah Hurwitz.
⁸ Adapted from Ps. 80:5; Lam. 2:13.
⁴ Lam. 2:1.
⁵ Num. 23:10.
⁶ Is. 57:1.
⁷ Based on Ps. 38:11.
⁸ The Vienna Jews, to which circle the Ries
family belonged, settled in Berlin after
their expulsion from Vienna in 1670.
⁹ Altona, although under the rule of Denmark, was governed by a President. Loeb
was safe in Altona from his Hamburg
creditors.
¹⁰ Esther 5:13.
¹¹ To «learn» Talmud (German—*lernen*) or
simply to «learn» means to give oneself to
the study and mastery of the Talmud,
Bible or other Hebraic lore. A pious Jew,
whatever his business or profession,

«learns» in all his spare time, throughout his life.

[12] The legalistic questions in the Talmud, together with their eleventh and twelfth century French-Jewish commentaries—altogether a stout curriculum for a lad of fourteen.

[13] Aaron ben Moses was murdered in the summer of 1687.

[14] The Jews were still living in Hamburg on sufferance.

[15] From Solomon Ibn Verga's chronicles, *Shebet Yehuda,* chap. 16. The anecdote refers to the charge of ritual murder often brought against the Jews at Passover season.

[16] Lev. 26:44.

[17] Samson Wertheimer of Worms (1658-1724), financier, purveyor, and court Jew to Leopold I of Austria. When Oppenheimer was absent from Vienna, Wertheimer represented his interests, and upon his death became court banker in his stead. But wiser than his associate, Wertheimer did not loan the greater part of his gains to the Austrian court, but invested them in land and houses. Ten soldiers stood as sentinels before his own residence in Vienna, and he was known among his contemporaries as the «Jewish Kaiser.» He was a learned Talmudist, and was instrumental in establishing a score of con-

gregations in the Austrian Empire. The court invested him with the title and authority of Chief Rabbi of Hungary. He not only secured a satisfactory dowry for his nephew in helping arrange the match with Glückel's son, but he managed to do as much or better for the Emperor Leopold by eliciting a dowry of one million florins from the King of Poland when the latter's daughter married Leopold's brother-in-law.

[18] Gen. 45:5.

[19] Prov. 19:21.

[20] Samson Baiersdorf (Samson Solomon ben Judah Selka—died, 1712), originally from Vienna, was the most famous of the court Jews of Kulmbach-Bayreuth. As factor to Margrave Christian Ernst of Brandenburg-Bayreuth, he was one of the most influential Jews of South Germany. The synagogue he built in Baiersdorf still stands with its old hangings and candelabra intact. His sons, with whom Glückel spent a merry evening at a village inn, later lost most of the family fortune and spent a considerable while in prison, due to false charges brought against them by a renegade Jew.

[21] Glückel here uses the common expression *Hof-Jude* (court Jew) for the court factor. Almost every king, prince, and dukelet in Central Europe had his court Jew

to whom he confided his business affairs.
Their character and careers have been made
popular in the unlucky person of Jew
Süss, the hero of Leon Feuchtwanger's
novel *Power*. Judah Berlin, Leffmann
Behrens, Samuel Oppenheimer, Samson
Wertheimer, Samuel Lévy and Samson
Baiersdorf were all court Jews, and enjoyed
powers and privileges far above the com-
mon run of their people.

[22] Meat and wine are not permitted during
the first nine days of the month of Ab
(save Sabbaths), in preparation for the
ninth day which commemorates the Fall
of Jerusalem.

[23] Allusion to Num. 27:21.

[24] Anschel Wimpfen died in 1697, which
year will serve to date the entire episode.

[25] Ecc. 8:8.

[26] The last will and testament of Abraham
ben Sabbatai Hurwitz of Prague, edited
with commentary by his brother, Jacob
(not Isaiah, as Glückel says). This type of
composition, known as an «Ethical Will,»
plays an important part in Jewish literature, and is replete with moral wisdom.
The English reader is recommended *Hebrew Ethical Wills* (Jewish Publication
Society, Philadelphia, 1926), two volumes
of selections, with translations, edited by
Israel Abrahams. I have omitted Glückel's

excerpt from Hurwitz in the fear that the «honey» may have lost its sweetness for the modern palate.

[27] Mordecai, the son of Moses ben Loeb, who married Glückel's daughter Freudchen, moved to London and enriched himself in the trade with India. He founded at London the Hambro congregation in 1702, the synagogue of which was built in 1725.

[28] The Oppenheimers were arrested on false charges in September, 1697.

Book Six

[1] Probably a slip of the pen for «eleven» years.

[2] The quotation is from the *Sayings of the Fathers*, II, 15, and the gloss following it is from the Talmud, *Shabbat*, 153-a.

[3] Cerf (Hirz) Lévy was the foremost banker of Lorraine.

[4] I Sam. 16:7.

[5] Prov. 19:21; and adaptation from Ps. 2:4.

[6] Job 3:25.

[7] Ecc. 1:9.

[8] Nearly seven weeks lay between the 1st of Nisan, the day set for her son's marriage, and Lagbeomar, the date of her own wedding. Her inquietude appears to be due to the uncertainty of when her son's wedding will actually be celebrated and her forebodings as to the fate of her money.

9 Glückel had met Abraham Krumbach on
the occasion of her daughter Esther's marriage to his son Moses. But she has chosen
to forget it.

10 Adapted from Song of Songs, 2:17.

11 Based on Num. 27:21.

12 Allusion to Ps. 2:11.

13 Ex. 15:26.

14 The favourite prayer of Jewish parents for
their male offspring. A linen band em-
broidered with the prayer and the child's
name is often presented to the synagogue,
where it is used to bind together the scrolls
of the Law.

15 The story of the city of Lus where no man
dies, is told in the Talmud, *Sota*, 46-b.

16 Ps. 139:7.

17 II Sam. 12:23.

18 Is. 57:1.

19 Ezek. 36:25.

Book Seven

1 Job 9:12.

2 Advocate and intercessor for the Jews in
their relations to public opinion and to
church and state authorities. Almost every
court Jew and prominent Jewish banker
acted as *schtadlan* in behalf of the Jews
of his land. Since the mass of the Jews had
no recognized rights as subjects or citi-
zens, they were dependent on the public

or secret influence of the *schtadlan* to secure them even a limited measure of
justice.

[3] The War of the Spanish Succession
(1701-14).

[4] Glückel does not altogether fulfill this
promise. After achieving the rank of court
Jew to Duke Leopold-Joseph of Lorraine,
Rabbi Samuel Lévy became, on January 1,
1716, minister of finance to the duchy.
By December of the same year he was
forced to resign; a few months later he
was sent to prison, together with his wife,
and although she was soon released, he
languished five years behind the bars, and
was released a broken and poverty-stricken
man. Being a court Jew or a Jewish minister of finance was a highly dangerous profession. For details, see *Revue des Études
Juives*, vol. 65, p. 274 and suite.

[5] Probably the governor of Metz.

[6] Upper Lorraine, including Lunéville, was
not united to the French crown until
1766, long after the present episode. Lower
Lorraine, including Metz, had belonged to
France since 1556. Moses Rothschild (or
Alcan), who opted to remain in Upper
Lorraine, was fined, together with other
Jews, 300 livres for standing at the window
of a hotel in Nancy smoking a pipe while
a procession of the Holy Sacrament passed

by—date May, 1711. The proprietor was forbidden thereafter to rent his front rooms to Jews. The following year Rothschild (or Alcan) went to prison for shipping Lorraine money to Metz.

7 Cerf Lévy died July 24, 1712.

8 Glückel's youngest daughter eventually married the son of Isai Willstadt.

9 Nikolsburg (Moravia) was one of the foremost Jewish communities of Central Europe, in the eighteenth century.

10 Schudt, a contemporary Christian writer on *Jewish Curiosities*, describes Rabbi Abraham Broda as a tall, powerfully built, and impressive man.

11 Is. 26:20.

12 Jewish women are required by the Law to keep their hair covered from view.

13 Lev. 26:36.

14 The Feast of Weeks, or Pentecost, celebrates the giving of the Law on Sinai.

15 Ps. 79:4.

16 Jonah 1:7.